THE CHILD AND THE STATE

This book is published as part of the joint publishing agreement established in 1977 between the Fondation de la Maison des Sciences de l'Homme and the Press Syndicate of the University of Cambridge. Titles published under this arrangement may appear in any European language or, in the case of volumes of collected essays, in several languages.

New books will appear either as individual titles or in one of the series which the Maison des Sciences de l'Homme and the Cambridge University Press have jointly agreed to publish. All books published jointly by the Maison des Sciences de l'Homme and the Cambridge University Press will be distributed by the Press throughout the world.

Cet ouvrage est publié dans le cadre de l'accord de co-édition passé en 1977 entre la Fondation de la Maison des Sciences de l'Homme et le Press Syndicate of the University of Cambridge. Toutes les langues européennes sont admises pour les titres couverts par cet accord, et les ouvrages collectifs peuvent paraître en plusieurs langues.

Les ouvrages paraissent soit isolément, soit dans l'une des séries que la Maison des Sciences de l'Homme et Cambridge University Press ont convenu de publier ensemble. La distribution dans le monde entier des titres ainsi publiés conjointement par les deux établissements est assurée par Cambridge University Press.

THE CHILD AND THE STATE

The Intervention of the State in Family Life

PHILIPPE MEYER

Translated by
JUDITH ENNEW
and
JANET LLOYD

CAMBRIDGE UNIVERSITY PRESS
Cambridge
London   New York   New Rochelle   Melbourne   Sydney

EDITIONS DE
LA MAISON DES SCIENCES DE L'HOMME
Paris

Published by the Press Syndicate of the University of Cambridge
The Pitt Building, Trumpington Street, Cambridge CB2 1RP
32 East 57th Street, New York, NY 10022, USA
296 Beaconsfield Parade, Middle Park, Melbourne 3206, Australia
and Editions de la Maison des Sciences de l'Homme
54 Boulevard Raspail, 75270 Paris Cedex 06

Originally published in French as *L'enfant et la raison d'état* by Editions du
Seuil, Paris, 1977, and © Editions du Seuil 1977

First published in English by Editions de la Maison des Sciences de
l'Homme and Cambridge University Press 1983 as *The Child and the State.
The Intervention of the State in Family Life*. English translation © Maison des
Sciences de l'Homme and Cambridge University Press 1983

Printed in Great Britain at
the University Press, Cambridge

Library of Congress catalogue card number: 83–2064

British Library cataloguing in publication data
Meyer, Philippe
The child and the state.
1. Family policy – France
I. Title   II. L'enfant et la raison d'etat.
English
362.8'256'0944   HQ623

ISBN 0 521 24871 X hard covers
ISBN 0 521 27035 9 paperback
ISBN 2 7351 0061 8 hard covers (France only)
ISBN 2 7351 0062 6 paperback (France only)

Fried. 29,50/26,55/1/26/84

CONTENTS

v

I

FAMILY REGULATIONS

The harm people suffer by living in an overpopulated society has been mended by its management, such is the power of order to modify this strange human disposition and compensate for nature. The gardener, in other words the government, has been seen to be taking care of his seed and concerning himself with future generations. (Sébastien Mercier, *Tableau de Paris*, 1781)

In its task of managing society, of devising and diffusing a single, secular and compulsory way of life, the State proceeds like a gardener. Amid a profusion of different ways of life, it is constantly clipping, rooting out, planting, pollarding, pruning, grafting, taking cuttings, planting trees, thinning out, fencing in, tending, planting out, laying waste, botanising, tilling the soil, landscaping, and distinguishing the crops from the purely ornamental plants.

The image conjured up by the word 'family' today is a structure which has been moulded from a mixed bag. The mixture is one of adults and children, of relatives and strangers, of married couples and single people, of vagrants and settled inhabitants, of the occupied and the unemployed, of masters and apprentices, the mixture in which all essential affective and social exchanges were carried on, at least until the eighteenth century. Philippe Ariès has shown the extent to which the child is a recent invention as the central individual in the organisation of the family, and how closely the private nature of family life corresponds with the transformation of the town.[1]

Without doubt, one can say that the present family came into being when society lost the street as the 'seat of business, of professional life, but also of gossip, conversation, entertainment

and games ... the familiar setting for social relations'.[2] When
the monarchy, having achieved political unity, turned to social
engineering, the first place to which it applied itself was the
town. When Richelieu built his ideal city on the borders of
Touraine and Poitou, his plan was one of ordered space,
modelled by the social monarch–architect; and reasons of State
were imposed upon

those ancient cities ... which are so badly constructed in comparison
with those which are regularly laid out on a plain by a surveyor who
is free to follow his own ideas ... that it might be said that it was
chance rather than the will of men guided by reason that led to such
an arrangement.[3]

The 'Reformation', or regulation of the town, was conducted by Colbert and, from 1667, by the first lieutenant of
police, La Reynie. When military operations demolished the
Court of Miracles thirty thousand 'vagrants' were driven out.[4]
The elevations of Paris were flattened, the mound of Saint-
Roche sheared off, houses set in rows and numbered, streets
redesigned and illuminated, monumental buildings used for
the organisation of traffic and to determine social functions.
Institutions were opened to confine or clear away those who
did not have 'either fixed abode or certain trade'. A town
scheme was drawn up. From being the common space, the
general locus of social life, the street was to become a place with
a single function, dedicated to traffic. From being an inhabited
area, it would become a crossing area, a place of transit. The
transformation of the town began with the clearing out of what
Restif de La Bretonne calls 'the streets of brotherly love where
two persons who met could not pass without embracing'.[5]
Devoted to traffic – kept on the move if possible – the street
became the object and terrain of control, an axis of repression
and penetration on the part of a 'well organised policing'
which 'allows the first magistrate to know more things about a
citizen than could be known to either his neighbours or those
who most regularly visited his house'.[6] The establishment of
the town within a space that could be standardised was thus
achieved through what Bentham calls 'the simple means of

architecture',[7] and its conversion into an organised space by means of penetrating and occupying the terrain.

In the new urban order, the family was to be amputated, relieved of its environment. Left to itself, it alone would increasingly have to fulfil the functions assumed, not so long ago, in the street, by society. Children previously used to learn to live in the midst of urban and social diversity. In other words, the transmission of knowledge and culture was effected by direct apprenticeship, by osmosis. The child was not separated from the community, but took part in its activities and made his own contribution to its rhythm; but that means that, not set apart as a member of a particular age group, neither did he particularly belong to any one couple. In the undiscriminating sociability of the street, the child scarcely belonged to anyone – *res nullius* – because he more or less belonged to everyone. Education and instruction were passed on directly by parents, but equally by masters and workshop companions, by neighbours and tradesmen in the street, and by those who lived under the same roof; for the house was not the dwelling place of one exclusive family unit.

The new disposition of the town established the division between public and private space; the State appropriated the first, restricting spontaneous sociability to the second, in which blood ties took on a new importance. The home now tended to become a substitute for the street, the new centre of life, a residence for family members only. The field of the child's affective and social involvement was little by little reduced to the conjugal family which, for its part, 'began to give to [the child] such importance that it lost its anonymity'.[8]

To be sure, this retreat from sociability, this turning in on itself of the family, and its resulting reorganisation around the child initially affected only the minority of those who were bringing about the economic and political transformations and deriving profit from them. The nobility entrusted with public responsibilities, living close to the king or representing him in the provinces, had broken their primordial relationship with the fief and the land, and were rooting themselves in the State;

as were the financial and manufacturing part of the bourgeoisie, for whom the State was the principal supplier and the principal client. In this process of reorienting their social situation, both these groups discovered private life and began to experiment with the family, that is to say with new domestic practices, a new delimitation of affective space, a new classification of relationships and new ways of organising the home. Abandoning the apprenticeship system, this lay clergy, and this State clientele, adopted the mode of instruction of religious practitioners (the college), where a boarding system and discipline would soon define a new manner of being and behaving.

But although the slow transformation of the family, focused upon the child, began among the elite of those with authority the model of that lifestyle became progressively influential. The rationalisation of towns caused a contraction in the space of social exchange. Without a suitable terrain within which to operate there were fewer possibilities for initiating and developing direct relationships, and this left the field free for institutions; the transmission of social manners, for example, was effected more and more through the mediation of the school.

Whether uprooting untidy weeds – vagabonds, beggars, the homeless and other 'irregulars' – or devising a space ordered in such a way as to exclude some people, keep others on the move, and set up yet others as ideal models, the State's social gardening operation was chiefly carried out by magistrates, the army and the police.

These men were, above all, town planners, town arrangers, the health inspectors of social life. Streets were gouged out but also cleaned; hospitals were built, but 'insanitary' districts were also destroyed. Berryer, Sartine and Lenoir were the precursors of Haussmann, Lépine and Chiappe.[9] They were the organisers of public space and of its management. In 1802 the Ministry of the Interior set up a Paris Sanitation Committee, soon to become the more powerful Health Committee. Hygiene was a matter for the police; a matter of law and order.

In a Paris which still reached only as far west as the Étoile, east to Père Lachaise, north to the Place Clichy and south as far as Montparnasse, the State laid out a 'healthy' centre, occupied by national buildings, aristocrats, bourgeoisie and their servants, prosperous artisans and their workmen, the employees of the administration, teachers etc. Inside the private mansions and bourgeois properties, each family lived in its own particular apartment.

On the ground floor, the porter's lodge where he plies his profession of tailor; on the first floor ... a luxurious apartment; on the second, the apartment of a bourgeois household (a musical composer) with children; on the third a painter and in the attic a young woman working through the night, beside her sleeping infant.[10]

These increasingly inward-looking families looked after their own homes and brought up their offspring there until they reached school age. Reception rooms, rooms for eating and sleeping; each one was given a function and to mix them was a sign of vulgarity. The roles of individuals within the family separated and became specified. The practice of jointly carrying out a trade disappeared, and this exaggerated the differentiation of the sexes; inside the apartment, which had become the essential area, the woman 'kept house', that is to say she set up, arranged and administered the family.[11]

Close to this organised centre, but like a different world, curving, scrubby, disordered, formless, the suburbs sheltered the lumpenproletariat. Water-carriers, rag-and-bone men, milliners, small shopkeepers, masons, carpenters, draymen and dockers, lived in the garrets and lodgings of Maubert or La Petite Pologne: 'the country of ten centimes a night of all the organ grinders, monkey show-men, acrobats and chimney sweeps who swarm on the pavements of the town'.[12] Poor overcrowded people: those who were decimated by the cholera epidemic of 1832; the boisterous populace that invaded the bourgeois *quartiers* on carnival days; the mutinous populace of the six thousand barricades of 1830. These inhabitants of the suburbs still lived a life of many-sided sociability, in the street with its free company and its taverns. But the more the town of the wealthy spread, the more the territory of the society of the suburbs shrank, wedged in by ancient barriers, then by the fortifications raised by Thiers in 1841. Whether bachelors or fathers of families, provincials were coming to Paris in ever greater numbers. Louis-Philippe's policy of public works and monumental building, the railway scheme adopted in 1837 by his government, the building fever and the 'craze for mortar', brought masons, carpenters, painters, roofers and workmen of all sorts to the capital, to swell the ranks of the people in the suburbs. Profusion degenerated into overcrowding, poverty into destitution. 'In one cramped hovel, which had an area of only two metres by three, including the stair-well, lived four people in two beds: an aged man, a woman, one girl of eighteen and a little one of five.'[13] Martin Nadaud mentions sixty people living in the same lodgings and reports that, in the Les Halles *quartier*, the population distribution was over 1,000 inhabitants per hectare.[14]

Although people lived according to the family order in the smart *arrondissements* of the capital, the people in the meaner *quartiers* lived in more or less indistinct tribal groups which were not divided into families by either cultural habits or material advantages. In this archaic social situation, one incompatible with industry, swarming in growing misery and seething with revolt, this increasingly congested population constituted the 'social problem'. The question of the capacity of the State to knit a society together was in effect being posed even as early as the 1830s, in studies devoted to the people of the suburbs and in the analyses of Guépin and Villeneuve-Bargemon and, later, those of Villermé, as well as in the novels of the 1840s, such as *Les Mystères de Paris*,[15] all of which recorded the confusion brought about by industrialisation.

The government, various academies, businesses and philanthropy all laid claim to the multitude and to a devotion to save them. Official charity, real compassion, statistics and study all combined with speculation (also very real) and the industrial boom, to increase massive intervention on the part of the State. It involved simultaneously systematising the struggle against disease, relieving poverty, redeeming areas for speculation, preventing riots (and repressing those which had not been foreseen and forestalled) and accustoming to work and factory rhythms a population which lived by the rhythm of the street. This enterprise took on the dimensions of a colonial war. It had its swordsmen, its looters, its missionaries and its nurses; it made use of stethoscope and pickaxe, tribunal and trowel, both in the academies where it was organised and in the suburbs where it took effect.

'The urban landscape acquires to an epic quality'[16] and that epic is from this point onwards *industrial*. Under the prefect Chabrol, new *quartiers* were begun in the west and north, which under the July monarchy became the fashionable part of the town: the Madelaine, Europe, Saint-Georges, and Monceau were built on areas that were for the most part vacant. The old town was disemboweled; Haussman, made prefect in 1852, had the wall of the Fermiers Généraux pulled down,[17] created the boulevards Saint-Germain, Saint-Michel and Sébastopol, designed the Champs-Élysées and the Étoile with its dozen branches, cleared the Place d'Italie, the Place de la Nation and the Place de la République and transformed the Île de la Cité. Under the new town he installed 800 kilometers of water pipes, 420 kilometers of sewers; and he raised 32,000 gas lamps. So crowded were the suburbs, and so massive their physical resistance to this official geometry, that it took fifteen years to raze *la butte des Moulins* and lay out the avenue linking the new Opéra and the gates of the Louvre.

On the first of January 1860, seventeen *communes* were annexed to Paris by imperial decree. 'Just imagine, we have become Parisians' exclaimed two peasants from Montmartre or Charonne, or Ménilmontant or Batignolles in a Daunier cartoon.[18] Every building that went up was subjected to rules, whether it was the height of houses, of apartments, and of roofs; or projections into the streets; the imperial decrees show the approach of a surveyor.

On the ruins of the former suburbs and in the fields of the annexed *communes*, private and public capital now created living space for the working class. The Napoléon housing estate, Rue Rochechouart, divided 600 people among two hundred dwellings, with the safeguard of a list of regulations running to more than a hundred articles. At Grenelle, Batignolles and Vaugirard, the Ville de Paris granted building-sites to private companies for the erection of 'workers' housing estates. 'Industrial premises' such as those erected in the suburb of Saint-Antoine, were an attempt to gather workmen together around their place of work. In 1889, Jules Siegfried and Georges Picot founded the *Société de l'habitat à bon marché* (Cheap Housing Society). In 1894, a law provided for, and organised, grants for this type of enterprise, which were increasingly numerous: the Society for Workers Housing, the Society for the Economic Housing of Large Families, etc. Major bourgeois dynasties created foundations specialising in cheap housing; the Rothschild or Singer-Polignac foundations for example, which frequently also financed hospitals and dispensaries.

Forms of social engineering multiplied. While the razing of the suburbs to the ground and the depopulation of the working-class *quartiers* were forging ahead, a policy for populating the spaces thus created as well as the new built-up areas was developed. This process of repopulation began with the organisation of an area of constraint, where the bourgeois mode of life was the constant point of reference and objective. The worker's apartment – a replica at the lowest level of the bourgeois home – was planned in such a way as to set the conjugal family apart, just as the apartment block became the 'dwelling place of a good paterfamilias' – as is still prescribed today in certain tenancy agreements. Conquerors and colonisers, the builders of the workers' housing estates and cheap apartment blocks could not imagine any model of life other than their own. Their architectural aims were to make families separate and private. The apartment block now suffered the same fate as the street: it became a space of public order. The new-found respectability of the status of proletarian environment compounded the loss in the workers' housing estate with the loss of craft in industrial labour.

In the vicinity of such housing estates as well as around working-class *quartiers* all vagrants were subjected to harassment by the police and the law. Under the Second Empire, the *gendarmerie* alone detained an average of 15,000 vagabonds a year. Employers refused to hire single workers and combatted every type of instability, of refusal to adapt to the industrial rhythm. The police force battled against places sheltering dubious types; 'furnished lodgings' and other 'transitional dwellings'. It controlled the taverns, *cabarets* classified in philanthropic imagery alongside hell. From 1872, all retailers of alcoholic drinks were required to hold a licence – which was under the control of the police. All public meeting places were subjected to regulations, even the fairs and markets which were considered 'prejudicial to morality and family well-being'.[19]

Social Economy, which Le Play defined as 'the science which seeks the causes of happiness for man not simply in wealth and form of government, but principally in social and moral development' – is a total economy. Time does not escape it any more than space does, nor work any more than leisure. The struggle to impose a day of rest on Sunday was added to the struggle against the *cabarets*. Workers preferred a 'Holy Monday' or even a holy week, so little integrated into the industrial rhythm were they and so much opposed to the new rationality.

The workers who earn the highest wages are those who practise economy the least, not only because they are absent from work on Monday, but because often they only return to their place of work after two or three days' absence when they have exhausted their resources.[20]

Now,

from the point of view of the working class, how can one deny the advantage of a day devoted to sociability which the State has the right, or even the duty, to fix, because if each one chose it according to his whim, he would harm the work of others, which has to be co-ordinated with his own?[21]

So Monday, the day for workers to enjoy together, was replaced by the bourgeois Sunday with the family.

'With the family' was the watchword of the whole range of moral advisors. It was the only condition, the only positive state produced by the industrial epic, and also the only one tolerated by it. Among the working-class population, necessity and common traditions made work everyone's affair – men, women and children alike. Philanthropists, who were also entrepreneurs and politicians, such as Jules Simon (a philosopher of the École Normale Supérieure, who was a State Deputy, Councillor of State, Minister, President of the Council, life senator, member of the Académie Française, sponsor of the Musée Social and founder – among other things – of the École Spéciale d'Architecture), specified the form and content of the family, by obtaining the imposition of increasingly strict regulations on work for women and children. Now work for children was not in itself either an innovation or a scandal. It became both when children were separated from adults yet constrained to do work similar to theirs, and when the framework of production was substituted for the framework of apprenticeship.

The link established between the question of housing and that of female and child labour formed the basis of the division of the proleteriat into families, and made it possible to draw a line between the regular and the irregular. The distribution of men to the factory, women to the hearth and children to school, was inseparable from the hunting down of the unmarried and those living in sin.[22] The policy of selection through repression matched and combined with one of attraction through money, and a quasi-monopoly over the distribution of work and housing. Despite the failure of workers' housing estates and industrial barracks, the more flexible policy of cheap housing, detached houses and rented property which eventually prevailed, multiplied the number of 'apartments', which with their built-in constraints necessarily promoted the organisation of family life on a private basis.

Once their subsistence was assured, families withdrew upon themselves in the interior of these spaces, and in some cases lost all patience with their role as educators, which the establishment of compulsory education had defined as an essentially instrumental function. 'We cry "to school" as our fathers used to say "to arms"' Jules Simon once exclaimed.[23] The fact is that it is indeed now a matter of raising children *en masse*. School is not simply one aspect among others of a child's education; it was conceived from the start as the foremost and, ultimately, the only one. Its timetables occupy the child's whole day; its programmes encourage indirect knowledge to the detriment of experience even where practical training is concerned; its discipline defines the ideal behaviour of a child in terms of passivity and blind obedience under an educational system of intimidation.

What then remains of the direct transmission of cultures, indeed of the cultures themselves? Many fragments remain, but frequently these are considered shameful,[24] and identified with poverty. 'Family feeling and sociability were not compatible and one could not develop without damage to the other.'[25] The State's work of unification and social standardisation is without doubt a slow process, but, by the last quarter of the nineteenth century it was already so well advanced, so apparently irreversible, that the family, the fundamental stereotype, was in a position to become the object of regulations. A regular marriage, stability of employment for the man, the wife's presence in the home, the children sent to school, separation from the social community and moderation in the family's *mores*, such are the standards of *homo industrialis*, and they are also those by which his standing is measured.

The substitution of an official form of social conduct for the cultures of a population reputed by the enthusiastic builders of the State's social policy to be without culture was achieved through the development of a code of children's rights. The child had become the essential part of the family, its most precious burden. The proliferation of control procedures for indigents, and for the regulation of parental authority, defined the child's rights as the index of family duties. In the war waged by the State against irregular families (those too sociable or given to producing unacceptable needs) the child is no more than a pretext and a hostage. Parental authority is an

instrument distributed by the State, which the State consequently has the power to retract. The absolute weapon of those
who inspect how families run their lives is to take away, or
threaten to take away, the children. All children who are
'guilty' or 'unhappy' or 'irregular' or 'neglected', to use the
expressions most current in the mouths of philanthropists,
come from a poorly kept family; 'the child in the street, the
future vagrant or thief becomes what he does become, in most
cases, through the parents' fault'.[26]

The contribution of the social sciences towards an understanding of *homo familialis*, and similarly of industrial society
(an understanding as exterior to the one as it is to the other),
afforded the regulation of the family a precision and an
authority which both public health and morality had failed to
provide. Psychology and sociology can elaborate a set of
instructions for family life and at the same time provide a series
of criteria of deviation.

By observing all the movements of industrial workers, Taylor
was able to eliminate those which he qualified as useless because
they did not contribute to the work. Likewise the social sciences,
by observing the totality of individual or group behaviours,
have decided which elements are functional, eliminating all
those which have no rational role in the private life of the family.
If the child is the essential element in these constructions and in
the social policies which stem from them, this is above all
because the process of the privatisation of life and of the
standardisation of families has reached its peak. Turned back on
themselves, enclosed in their own apartments, families are now
feasting affectively and emotionally upon themselves.

With its very functions delegated by the State, and able to
exercise them only under State supervision, the family finds its
activity limited to escorting its progeny to the institutions which
have established a monopoly over apprenticeship, health, sport
etc. The specific characteristics of the child, which follow
inevitably from the transformations undergone by the environment and work in general, are exacerbated by all this State
machinery. Competitiveness is the general rule, and first and

foremost in school. But competition also extends to all aspects of life inseparable from the birth of the family. The more the range of social models is actively limited by the State, the more class differences depend only on degree, on variations within a single model, and the more acutely felt and intolerable they become.

In so far as only one model remains, namely that of the bourgeois environment, any deviation from it is not only a peculiarity or failure to observe the conventions: it is a symptom of sub-humanity. In so far as only one space for living exists, namely that of the family, any escape from it, by accident or design, is a derangement. A return to order can only be achieved through the family, perhaps by the runaway returning to make a vow of allegiance, perhaps by therapists and magistrates redefining the family configuration *ad infinitum:* displacing one of its members, withdrawing another, replacing the missing member, or restoring him or her in make-believe. In stereotyped residential units spread throughout the stereotyped urban environment, the family stereotype only appears viable by virtue of the State's constant endeavours: orthopaedics 'to correct contrary conciousness'[27]; prosthetics in 'the help given to domestic authority by grafting on to it the support of public authority'[28]; surgery in eliminating families of contagion; zoology in observation of the species; genetics in the control of mutations. If the machinery of the law has been, at least until recent times, the distributor and the adaptor through which the medical, social, scientific and policing activities all work together in these endeavours, it has done so primarily through outlawing vagrants, formally condemning vagrancy and exploiting the secular power of parental authority.

All of this makes the contemporary family appear as the residue from the State's unceasing labours to limit options, destroy sociability and atomise society. The glorious creation of social 'gardening' on the part on the public authorities, to wit the family – celebrated as the 'fundamental unit of society' – seems to represent a passing phase in the long, devastating process of the impoverishment of the life of the community.

2

THE REALM OF OFFICIAL RECOGNITION

Vagabondage usually indicates the first step in a career which ends in prison, or occasionally on the scaffold; vagabondage is to the apprentice what prostitution is to the working girl, it is a sort of declaration of independence, it is the first act of defiance against the social order.[1]

Vagrants are people without allegiances. Although there have been all manner of vagrants and of vagrancies, though vaga-bondage alone or in a group, has served all sorts of social functions, though there have been all sorts of repressions or recaptures, vagabonds and escapees, there is really only one definition of vagrancy that remains valid across time and across space: it is that vagrants are people without allegiances. In the context of feudal rights, the vagrant is one who makes no oath of allegiance, one who pays no homage, one who recog-nises no overlord, and is claimed by no lord, one who thus settles nowhere, asks for no protection and has no claim to any. His wish is not to depend on any man; his risk is that he is neither protected nor recognised by any other. He takes what he can and what he wishes from social life, until he settles down, or is made to settle down.

It was in order to loosen such bonds of allegiance and all the impositions that they implied that serfs banded together and went wandering, after the 1146 crusade. Their ranks were swelled by those ruined by that expedition, by isolated wander-ers, by robbers of all kinds. These large roving bands of peasant-slaves were a response to the great movement towards Jerusalem, an attempt to shake off the yoke. They were soon tamed. At the end of the century, around 1180, groups of 'mercenaries' formed who put themselves at the service of one lord or another, often against their former masters, to set about the conquest and pillage of a region. A carpenter, named Durand, raised the Brotherhood of Peace, a sort of popular army, against them, and wiped them out in 1183 at Dun-le-Roy. But soon these itinerant seekers-after-justice turned against their lords hoping to punish those who held to feudalism; and the Brotherhood of Peace, in its turn was decimated.

Later, when the Turkish conquest was devastating the Byzantine Empire, bands of Bohemian, Egyptian and Hungarian gypsies criss-crossed the roads of Europe with varying success. With each famine, privations drove more mobs of all kinds into a life of chance and adventure; people such as the 'coquillards' (false pilgrims of St James) hierarchically organised for plunder and robbery. The universities attracted groups of roving students hoping to acquire their qualifications, at less cost and moving from Dole to Caen, from Nantes to Bordeaux, from Bourges to Valence. Poverty also had its faculties, where at least one of the thirty-six begging trades listed by the historians of the Court of Miracles could be learnt. More 'recognised' but no less itinerant trades such as those of the charcoal-burner or the woodcutter for instance, involved constant migrations and were sometimes violently repressed.[2]

With the advance of national unification, with each war, then with each colonial enterprise, the army was by one means or another increasingly absorbing those who were without hearth or home. In 1656, the Hôpital Général became the first place for the preventive detention of vagrants. The authorities tried to reduce the number by prohibiting first begging, then almsgiving. A royal decree of 1700 imposed a fine of fifty livres on each person caught giving to a beggar. Then again, a homeopathic treatment was applied to the aimless traveller: the final solution. Military expeditions were followed by or combined with colonial ones. On 12 May 1719, the Compagnie d'Occident was authorised to 'take young people of both sexes who had been brought up at La Pitié, at La Salpêtrière and at Les Enfants Trouvés, and to transport them to French

America'. It was deportation for the able-bodied, confinement for the inadequate.

In reality, the policy of La Reynie, by which the town was to be made perpetually administrable, presupposed the permanent elimination of the homeless. At the same time, by destroying certain *quartiers* and remodelling the town, it uprooted an enormous number of townspeople, leaving them without hearth or home and turning them into beggars and displaced persons. State intervention in the town, which primarily represented a considerable disruption, thus coincided with the beginning of a period of permanent intervention against the indigent and with a narrowing of the definition of what was conventionally acceptable; at the same time it ensured that an individual required an increasing number of predetermined characteristics to be publicly recognised. Policing, which was becoming the essential urban science, became the subject of a monumental three-volume treatise drawn up by de la Mare, La Reynie's deputy, and published to acclaim throughout Europe. The policed town is uninhabitable for those who cannot accommodate themselves to a steady trade and permanent domicile:

His Majesty has been informed that the great number of vagabonds and vagrants has been growing in the realm ... and that even natives of Paris or people who have lived there for many years, instead of being occupied in useful trades, seek and find their subsistence in shameful begging, which is equally contrary to good order and public peace; therefore His Majesty, wishing to take the necessary precautions and prevent the inconvenience which the sickness of some and the sloth of others could produce, has commanded, orders, wishes and expects:

Article 1: That eight days after the publication of the present decree all beggars and vagabonds, vagrants of either sex ... be obliged to return to the place of their normal habitation or to be employed in useful trades.

Article 2: That at the end of the said time, vagrants, vagabonds and other beggars be arrested and confined in the places set aside for them ... that those who are found to be able-bodied and of appropriate age be taken to the colonies and that they be confined until the day of their departure.

Article 3: And as it is fitting equally to charity and justice to confine, and to provide for the subsistence needs of those of the said beggars, who by their age and infirmities are not in a state to work, His Majesty orders that the paupers of this degree be forthwith confined in the hospitals which have already been established or that His Majesty will establish for this purpose, to remain there until such time as they are able to live without help from the public purse.

Article 4: His Majesty forbids all landlords and principal leaseholders of households in the town and suburbs of Paris, and all landlords of furnished rooms, to lodge and take in, either by day or by night, any individual of the estate before mentioned, on pain of disobedience and prison.

Article 7: His Majesty orders that the Military Criminal Lieutenant, and all the officers of the mounted police of the town of Paris and throughout the realm, give good assistance to arresting the said beggars, vagabonds and vagrants and forbids any person from hindering them in such arrests.

Article 8: The Police officers shall each month draw up a register of able-bodied vagrants and beggars ... and orders shall then be sent for them to be taken to the place from which they shall be deported.

Article 9: His Majesty forbids the said beggars, vagabonds and vagrants to group together or commit any violence, on pain of death.

Omnes civitates imperii debent sequi consuetudinem urbis:[3] while the town was thus patrolled and brought to heel the countryside was scattered with detachments, and the mounted police, previously a mobile force, now settled in. The Secretary of State for War, Le Blanc, split the mobile companies, usually based in the main town of the province, into regular squads posted in important villages situated on main routes 'in such a way that each of them should have four or five leagues to guard on each side'. In 1720, 565 squads mostly composed of five men, two of whom carried out the daily rounds, occupied and covered the territory 'in order to be able to answer for the stretches which they had to guard'. In the network of this 'general supervision' the mounted police spotted and rounded up the vagabonds, and distributed them in institutions set up for that purpose.

The Revolution tried to departmentalise these institutions by creating (mainly on paper) depots and shelters connected to (and reproductions of) the Hôpital Général. The Empire offered the army or prison. A decree of 5 July 1808, 'on the eradication of begging', punished beggars with a penalty of three to six months imprisonment, at the end of which they would be taken into a 'Poor House' where they would be given work. The third chapter of the penal code of 1810 went further, by establishing begging and vagrancy as 'Crimes and offences contrary to public order'. The elimination of vagrancy was accepted to be a continuous task and hunt. Vagrancy was an offence, a permanent infraction, punishable at all times: 'vagabonds or vagrants are those who have neither fixed abode nor means of subsistence and who do not habitually exercise any trade or profession'. Meanwhile, by resuscitating 'the plea of minority' a principle laid down in 1719, applicable to those under sixteen years of age, the code was already, albeit tentatively, proposing a right of exception for minors in connection with which the family would be given encouragement with positive ends in view. By giving the benefit of this excuse only to minors under sixteen who acted 'without discretion' the law was indicating the essential direction in which criminal law for children was to develop, attaching greater importance to the act than to the law, to the delinquent individual than to the offence itself, to the family than to the child.

When the vagrant under sixteen had acted without discretion, he was acquitted and, 'according to circumstances' returned to his parents or 'taken to a house of correction, there to be brought up and detained for such a number of years as the sentence determines, which shall, however, at no time exceed the period in which he attains his twentieth year'. If he had acted with discretion, he was to incur a prison sentence, which could not be more than half of that applicable to an adult for the same offence.

The plea of minority for children 'without discretion' departed from the general principles of the penal code in that it no longer had a prison sentence of determinate length corresponding to an equally determinate offence. All the efforts of the apostles of 'child delinquents' were to focus upon obtaining general acceptance for this dislocation between offence and sentence, this distinction between the delinquent and his crime. The gradual replacement of repression by re-education was to come about by as far as possible setting aside the fixed sentences of criminal law, by concentrating on the facts of the case rather than on the law, by having deprivation of liberty for a fixed time give way to a placement for an indeterminate period. Taking into care first delinquent minors and subsequently also 'minors at risk', was to be organised on the basis of that period being an extendable one and such jurisdiction being applicable to an ever-increasing number of cases.

This is the sense in which to understand the law of 28 April 1832, which provided that all vagrants under sixteen 'can not be condemned to the penalty of imprisonment, but ... will be discharged under the supervision of the high police until they reach the age of twenty, unless they contract a regular engagement in the army or naval forces before that age'. To be under the supervision of the high police, meant being obliged to inform the Ministry of the Interior of one's residence and telling it of all one's movements. As from 1851, it came to mean accepting the residence chosen for the vagrant by the administration; any infraction being punished by imprisonment or deportation to the colonies.

From 1832 to 1906, the legislation on the vagrancy of minors remained virtually unchanged, although convictions for vagrancy multiplied sevenfold between 1830 and 1896. But, practically speaking, there were many alterations in the repression of vagrancy. They came about under pressure exerted by the numerous philanthropic societies who were organising the taking of delinquent minors into care in the reform schools created in 1850, and flourishing during the second half of the nineteenth century. The pressures of these charitable societies were at first applied to obtaining a stricter policing control of vagrant minors and more severe judicial repression. Too many police superintendents were content to admonish the vagrant and then release him, and not to report the young delinquent to the public prosecutor. Too many prosecutors abstained from

bringing charges and too many judges from passing sentence.
What was needed was a wider definition of vagrancy than that
given by the code. Although jurisprudence had at first considered as vagrants only those who had *neither* fixed abode *nor*
means of subsistence, it should in future consider either of these
two conditions on its own to constitute an offence, and any
individual having the means of subsistence but no home, or *vice
versa*, to be a vagrant. Simultaneously, philanthropic societies
were fighting prostitution, considered to be a regular source of
vagrant income; and there were numerous campaigns for the
law to assimilate prostitution to vagrancy. The aim was to
include in the categories of minors liable to be taken into care,
all the troublemakers first in the factories and then in the
schools, whether or not the code provided for the repression of
their conduct, and to put an end to what the newspaper, *La
Providence*, called 'this disturbing craze for movement and
idleness [which] appears to be a feature that has survived from
the undisciplined life of the savage'. To civilise the savage, the
legalist-philanthropists proposed a 'justice of forethought and a
justice of repression'.[4]

This justice of forethought was to organise the collaboration
– or collusion – of judges, advocates, and prosecutors together
with the Committee for Defending Children brought before
Justice, during the whole of the last quarter of the nineteenth
century. This holy alliance fought to abolish the law of 1832,
and the 'intimidating and brutal' supervision of the high
police, for

true supervision is devoted, charitable, fraternal. [It is that of]
philanthropic societies, which act through material and moral
assistance, through affection and sympathy which penetrate the
inner spirit ... It is the best kind of supervision, and every day has the
most beneficial effects.[5]

Everyone involved set about producing these beneficial
effects.

When the minor goes before a preliminary investigation the president
of the bar always designates for his assistance an advocate member of
the Committee for Defending Children Brought before Justice. The

advocate communicates his intentions to the Committee, where the matter is discussed and the solution arrived at, and lastly he comes to an understanding with the philanthropic society in almost all cases where sentencing to correction is not judged necessary. Almost always, the examining magistrate or juvenile court magistrates are in agreement with the advocate and the Committee.[6]

The 1832 law in effect lapsed as a result of this daily collusion, which was able to circumvent its official rulings all the more easily given that those brought to trial did not use their right of appeal, if only because of their social origin. The vagrant child was surrounded by good intentions. Wherever he turned, he saw the same faces. Those who claimed to be working to defend him, were determined to 'sentence him in his best interests' and to that end enlisted powerful collaborators to help them. Thus in Toulouse in 1897, the Committee for Defending Children brought before Justice had, as its president, the senior president of the Court of Appeal, as vice-presidents the Attorney General and the President of the Bar, and as general secretary a professor of the Faculty of Law. Magistrates, advocates and academics in effect made up the majority of the members and, above all, of the administrators of the philanthropic societies concerned with the fate of the 'delinquent child'. Those who played no part at the moment of sentencing, managed the reformatories or busied themselves with the social reintegration of those set at liberty, working through such philanthropic societies as the French Union for Saving Children and Adolescents, the particularly important General Society of Prisons, the League for the Children of France, the Society for the Prevention of Begging by Children, the Society for the Support of Young Prisoners and Discharged Youth, the Society for the Protection of Volunteer Conscripts, brought up under administrative guardianship, etc. The aim of this last institution, created in 1878 by Félix Voisin, an ex-prefect of police, who became councillor at the Supreme Court of Appeal, was to encourage young delinquents to enlist voluntarily with the army. With paternal solicitude, it increased the gratuity they received upon enlistment, invested some of it in a savings bank, and increased the rate of interest on this investment. In 1900 it had under its protection 3,000 wards, only seventy-two of whom were again brought before the courts, 'while over 400 of them won promotion and some even received the military medal'.

This frenzy of taking into care, this burst of enthusiasm for 'true supervision', this benevolent protection, started with the court and even reached as far as service under 'military colours', turning the vagrant into a non-commissioned officer and also an investor. It was a double movement on the part of a group from the professional classes wishing to enhance its power and a State bent on designing society and policing industrialisation. The magistrates, the houses of correction, the philanthropic societies, gathered into their nets all those who, being over eight and under twelve years of age, were avoiding eight hours of daily factory work (or twelve hours if they were between twelve and sixteen). They also gathered in those who were playing truant from school. In 1889, 600,000 children, one-eleventh of the population that was of school age, were still unaffected by compulsory education. Philanthropists and magistrates wished to give them educational justice. This was the thin end of the wedge, leading towards taking the environment itself into care. If the State was giving apprenticeship a social function, it was in order to combat destitution. Public order meant not only an absence of unrest but assigning each individual to his proper place in society. Supervising this process was the role of the philanthropic societies, and it was one they were playing increasingly effectively. Thus in a circular of 31 May 1898, at the request of the Committee for Defending Children brought before Justice, Milliard, the Minister of Justice, urged the Attorney General to stop 'considering that certain offences committed by sixteen-year-old minors were not of sufficient interest to the public order to justify opening a regular legal proceeding'. He invited public prosecutors to bring charges in a systematic fashion, and examining magistrates to interest themselves in the capacities and the environment of the child as much as in his offence:

'judicial authority should never lose sight of the fact that in all questions directly affecting children, its essential role is to give its assistance to a work of raising moral standards and rehabilitation'.

By the beginning of the twentieth century there were thus more and more vagrant children being charged and more and more benevolent societies to take them into care for longer and longer periods. This repression, originally justified by the lack of any domicile or income, was now increasingly accounted for by the failure of the family environment, and the need to direct the child towards an institution of apprenticeship or towards work. To be a vagrant was no longer simply to be in the wrong.

In 1906, the age of legal majority was raised from sixteen to eighteen years, and the number of minors who could be affected by educative measures was accordingly increased. The notion of discretion was retained. Those who had given no proof of it profited from the rehabilitation measures; those who did show it were no longer placed under the supervision of the high police but were forbidden residence, usually in the departments where they had their home ties. This made compulsory vagrants of them. The law of 11 April 1908 classed prostitution as an offence: the philanthropists had triumphed. The law of 22 July 1912, which created special courts for juveniles, at the same time extended the application of measures of rehabilitation to all minors of thirteen years, now presumed irresponsible. The fixed term penalty was losing ground. For convicted minors between thirteen and eighteen years deemed to have acted without discretion, the law of 1912 was the source of important innovations: it created an intermediate measure between sending a child back to his parents and placing him in a reform school, namely committing him to a trustworthy third party or to a charitable institution. It might be supposed that this represented no more than ratification of the role of the private associations and the practices of collusion which I have described above. In reality, there was more to it: the application of the law revealed that the vagrants who were placed in charitable institutions were not those who before

1912 would have been sent to a reformatory but those who had
in those days simply been sent back to their families. It
constantly happens – even today – that new measures are
taken which, although purporting to provide a more humane
alternative for those for whom repression is most severe, in
reality introduce new possibilities of getting at those whom the
strictures of the law had not previously reached. Another
innovation that was to have a great future accompanied these
measures of intervention: the probation system. It was applied
to vagrants returned to their families who now, at the discretion of the probation officers, were to remain under judicial
control. It was the beginning of the pedagogic invasion of the
'natural milieu'.

The law of 24 March 1921, in its turn, had the effect of
setting an official seal upon a judicial practice to which I have
already referred, namely extending to the maximum the
conditions of application of articles 270 and 271 of the penal
code, by defining vagrancy as the absence of any fixed abode
and of any income. It would henceforth be possible for the law
to consider as vagrants, 'minors of 18 years who having,
without legitimate cause, quitted either their parents' home or
the places where they had been placed by the authority to
which they had been entrusted, had been found wandering or
living in lodgings and either not engaging regularly in any
profession or gaining their income from debauchery or illegal
occupations'. The insertion of the expression 'without legitimate cause' at the beginning of this text does not mean that the
legislator waived the right to take certain categories of vagrant
into care. The only vagrants 'with legitimate cause' were, in
fact, those who had fled the parental home because of the bad
treatment which they suffered there, and the law of 1921 only
made their flight legitimate in so far as the laws of 1889 and
1898 provided for the taking into care of 'unhappy children' of
this kind.

Following the law of 1921, where minors were concerned,
vagrancy became a much wider concept than that of the code
of 1810: raising the legal majority to eighteen years had

appreciably increased the number of those liable to legislation referring to runaways. The adoption of the principle of the non-responsibility of minors of thirteen years had extended the field for educative measures. The ratification of the role of charitable associations and the creation of the probation system tended towards the same effects. The concept of vagrancy was, in fact, a 'catch-all' notion which enabled the law to pounce upon the cases of all those who had committed no offence other than that of playing truant from school or industrial work. At the same time, the treatment meted out for vagrancy had taken a more pedagogical form, and placement for an indeterminate period had definitely taken the place of deprivation of liberty for a fixed period. The conjunction of these two decisions found ratification in the decree of 30 October 1935, which, by deciding (in the words of the Minister Louis Rollin) that 'vagrant children are above all unhappy children', removed the vagrancy of minors from the province of criminal law and assigned it to that of civil law: vagrant children were now 'civilised'.

Henceforth, vagrancy in minors was no longer a crime; the vagrant child needs protection, not reprimands, and the judge now had power to appraise the minor and his environment and could thereupon resort to a wide range of possibilities in placing the child. This marked a climax in the policing of families. The Vichy government concerned itself with child delinquency with its law of 22 July 1942; the provisional government of the Liberation then annulled that law, only to take the same measures in another of its own making. The measures were in effect in direct line with the decree of 1935, in that they looked ahead to the creation of centres of observation and guardianship 'where, before coming up for trial, minors would be submitted to physical and mental examinations bearing also upon their professional capacities'. The laws of 1945 and 1958 essentially retained these measures, moving towards the establishment of concrete means of control over families and psychiatric treatment for delinquent minors, or minors 'at risk'. All in all, the ambitions of the provisional government were very comprehensive: to detach the management of approved schooling from the penal administration and instead make it autonomous within the framework of the Ministry of Justice. The Ministry was to be entrusted first with the task of applying the decree of 2 February 1945 referring to child delinquency, which introduced profound changes in the criminal law for minors; secondly, with the preparation for recasting civil law (which was henceforth to include vagrancy) in order to produce a unified canon of the law affecting children. Before this task was started, the management of approved schooling undertook a critical analysis of existing legislation. On the score of vagrancy, the director and sub-director of approved schooling, J. L. Costa and P. Ceccaldi, took exception to the decree of the 30 October 1935 for 'not having explicitly recognised enquiries of a social nature and medical examinations to be just as necessary for vagrants as they are for delinquents',[7] and for 'not having sufficiently enlarged the concept of vagrancy and thus severely limited its application, despite all legal efforts'. They proposed to extend the concept to include 'children who tended to elude the authority of their parents, even though they continued in principle to live with them, or were practising a recognised profession'. In less than a century and a half, the legal conception of vagrancy both in theory and in practice had become a gigantic trap. In 1810 it was necessary, in order to be convicted, to have neither trade nor home. After 1908, in the legal texts, but well before this in practical jurisprudence, it was necessary that both trade and lodging should be recognised. The 1945 recommendations, which led to the rulings of 1958 and 1970, meant that it was possible to be a vagrant even with a fixed abode and an acknowledged trade. This was domiciled vagrancy.

The civil code had a name for this domiciled vagrant; it was 'a child in moral danger'. The progress of judicial intervention was extending constantly on all sides: an extension of the range of circumstances covered by the notion of vagrancy; an extension of the range of ways of taking into care and the diversification of such care (prison, special *quartier*, reformatory, probation), then, after 1958, Educational Assistance in an Open Environment (AEMO), an extension of the field of those taken into care (from the minor on his own, to the minor and his family, and then to the minor, his family and his environment); and finally an extension of the duration of the care, from a fixed duration to an indeterminate one up to the age of majority.

All movement of an uncontrolled nature was correspondingly proclaimed suspect. Judge Chazal, a pioneer in the introduction of the social sciences into legal practice, was disturbed by the fact that in the summer of 1960 'for 3,000,000 young urban dwellers of between fourteen and eighteen years of age, 1,074,000 months of vacation had been spent under the effective control of the family or of social bodies of one kind or another, as against 4,349,000 months of holiday free from all control, whether of a social or a family nature'.[8] The time for holidays was already institutionally fixed, but should now also be controlled. The large migrations of young holiday makers ought to be matched by large migrations of State Security Police (CRS), beach attendants, social organisers and leisure-time experts.

In the same period, the president of Équipes d'Action, Jean Scelles, published in the review, *Rééducation*, a little manual of good conduct and usage for drivers solicited by hitch-hikers:

a warning through the press against allowing minors into private cars and lorries is necessary, because the use of cars is general and minors (boys or girls) regularly resort to it in their many attempts to abscond from their families or from places of re-education. When a minor (boy or girl) hitches a lift, it is useful to ask for his or her identity in a precise manner (with the production of an identity card) and to inform the *gendarmerie*, for one must come to the aid of families of missing persons.[9]

From feeling alarm at the idea of holidays that spell liberty, to favouring a society of sycophants is a logical step to take. Just as there is no longer space without function, there is no longer time without control, nor movement without goal. Social life is given its final form: the entire social and geographical terrain has become a realm where official recognition is necessary.

3

THE STATE: HOME OF THE FAMILY

How public authority comes to the air of domestic authority (Félix Morin, *Des comités de défense des enfants traduits en justice*, 1879)

For many years domestic authority was undivided and so subject to neither judge nor arbitrator. Only the sovereign's authority – justified by its own naturally paternalistic character – was able to impose upon it limits such as the prohibition against putting one's own children to death. But it never attempted to regulate the modes of exercising the *patria potestas*, and it was to the father, and to the father alone, that family policing belonged. To be sure, the State could lend him assistance by putting its prisons at his disposal, where his rebellious children could be kept, but that was simply a kind of public service which involved no transfer of authority, no delegation of paternal power. The best-known procedure was that of a *lettre de cachet* (order under the King's Privy Seal). It was a secret procedure which the King alone could decide, and was reserved for fathers of the nobility. Families of meaner extraction could have their children shut away through the offices of a police lieutenant, under the, in most cases distant, control of magistrates and high courts.

In fact the first limitations set upon the exercise of this right of paternal correction stemmed from a decision by the High Courts to consolidate their power and exercise a real and rigorous control on social life. In the middle of the eighteenth century, the Attorney General of the High Court of Paris decided on an investigation into the institutions in which rebellious children were imprisoned (excluding the Bastille). It found a miscellany of young children knowing neither how to speak nor, in some cases, how to walk, placed there because they were an obstacle to the father's remarriage; ten-year-old children whose parents were defrauding them of their inheritances; and priests of a more or less rebellious nature, sent to prison through the paternal authority of their bishops. All would live out their days in an institution of confinement. The High Court of Paris accordingly decided to impose some regulations upon a father's right to punish. By a series of decrees passed in 1673, 1678, and 1697 it stipulated that remarried fathers could not cause their children to be detained except with the permission of the civil lieutenant; that children could not be detained after twenty-five years of age and that a special establishment should be created at Villeneuve-sur-Gravois in order to avoid mixing delinquents and rebellious children. But before long this regulation led to the introduction of differential treatment, according to the father's social origin; 'children of the working classes who misbehave towards their fathers and mothers, refuse to work through licentiousness or give themselves up to debauchery, may be incarcerated, the boys in Bicêtre until the age of 25 and the girls in La Salpêtrière'[1]. Unlike the children of the leisured classes, these poor children could not be removed from detention on the simple request of the father. Henceforth they belonged to the State. As for the treatment of 'young people of good family' this was specified in the decree of 15 July 1763:

Parents whose sons fall into behavioural disorders which could endanger the honour and tranquillity of their family, without however being guilty of crimes punishable by law, may request the Secretary of State for War and Marine Affairs that they be deported to the island of La Désirade. If the parents' motives are found legitimate, the young people will be taken to La Désirade by order of his Majesty ... There they will be submitted to a regime of supervision and work.

Those who mended their ways obtained a concession of land at Marie-Galante; later, if their family so desired, they were returned to France.

Thus if he obtained the King's consent, a noble father could shut up his son in the Bastille or his daughter in a convent and have them released when he thought fit. The bourgeois father had the possibility of sending his son to the islands, or causing him to be locked away until the age of twenty-five, with the authorisation of a civil lieutenant, but could also put an end to this 'deportation' or imprisonment. The poor father could have his son sent to Bicêtre. There he would remain until the age of twenty-five, provided the Compagnie d'Occident had not by then sent him to French America, as authorised by the decree of 12 May 1719. Such a father would at no time be able to revoke his decision. The first important measures for regulating parental authority were thus tried out on the poor classes.

The Revolution accentuated this trend towards imposing controls upon the exercise of paternal authority, by requiring a magistrate's approval in consigning a child to punishment. The lowering of the civil age of majority to twenty-one years furthermore restricted the number of children liable to be submitted to such measures[2]. The civil code of 1803 regressed, or rather adopted a mixed system of controls: children under the age of sixteen could be held in detention at their father's request for a maximum period of one month. The president of the court was obliged to sign the incarceration order in cases where the father made this request. The child could be imprisoned several times, on the condition that each imprisonment did not exceed one month. Children of between sixteen and twenty-one years could not be detained at their father's request, unless the president of the court consented, after consultation with the public prosecutor. In such a case, the imprisonment could not exceed a period of six months. But, as with the minor of under sixteen, this could be repeated after intervals of liberty. Up until 1850 the minor, whatever his age, was sent to the prison of his own particular department, exactly as if he had been condemned by a court of justice. The law of 18 August of that year stipulated that a special area in each prison be set aside for these young detainees. The father could cause the detention to end at any moment, whatever the age of his son.

Between 1830 and 1855, the number of those sent for

punishment multiplied fivefold[3]. It was particularly high in large towns such as Paris, Marseilles, Toulouse, Bordeaux, Rennes and Lyons. The exercise of the father's right of punishment was, in the great majority of cases, a feature of the poorer classes, to such an extent that Napoleon III's Minister of the Interior, Fialin de Persigny, wrote in a report to the Emperor dated April 1852:

It has been noticeable that, among certain needy and depraved parents, there is a fatal tendency to leave, or even place, their children under the provisions of these sentences where the benefits outweigh the disadvantages. They thus burden the State with the trouble of their education, only to reclaim them after a number of years, in order to profit from their work, often in the most shameful schemes. These deplorable calculations are due to the over-exclusive emphasis laid, over the past years, upon ideas of assistance and charity in the management of institutions for young detainees, and particularly in private establishments. The repressive character of punitive education is not felt strongly enough in the reformatories, which certain classes are beginning to consider as colleges for the poor.[4]

It was indeed the fact that 85 per cent of the children to whom the procedure of paternal correction was applied were the children of manual workers and journeymen, compared with only 2 per cent of children whose parents exercised one of the liberal professions. Furthermore the latter were confined in separate sections within the correctional establishments where, as for example at Mettray, tutors supervised their education, while the children of poorer classes were out working in the fields.

In the face of this attitude towards the procedure of confinement for paternal punishment on the part of the working classes, Fialin de Perisgny took measures 'to place girls exclusively in religious establishments, and to enlist all youths suitable to military service'. He added that 'the regiment for some and the convent for others constitutes a wholly organised patronage, and one which offers society the most reliable guarantees'.[5]

It was the start of a two-pronged movement. This consisted
on the one hand of discouraging the poorer classes from using
the procedure of paternal punishment and on the other hand of
fundamentally modifying the conditions of that practice in
order, eventually, to transform it. The work of dissuasion
started by Persigny bore fruit, and the number of demands for
paternal punishment stopped increasing after 1860 and stabilised at around 1,200 a year by the end of the century. As for
the work of modification and transformation, this was a task in
which magistrates and philanthropic societies joined forces to
run reform schools. The fact was that the judges soon ceased to
tolerate a situation in which the mere father of a family,
especially one from the lower classes, could obtain from them
the decision to send his child for punishment, their only power
being that of signing the detention order. In addition, the said
father of the family, in practice, tended to make such use of the
judge's decision as he pleased; many fathers, once the correction order had been signed, were content to keep it in their
possession simply to wave it in the air as a threat, without ever
implementing it. An equal number obtained a one-month
correction order from the president of the court and went to
reclaim their child after no more than a few days, being of the
opinion that the warning would have been sufficient; or they
demanded and obtained a six-month order, which for the same
reasons they brought to an end after a few weeks, as was their
right. Then there were, as Persigny had surmised, others who
exercised their right of correction to serve their economic
situation, by reason of their seasonal unemployment etc.
Neither the magistrates nor the philanthropists were satisfied
with this situation. They could not accept being exploited in
this way; besides, it was a matter of taking positive social
action, not of encouraging idiosyncratic behaviour.

To oppose the parents' freedom to use the right of punishment, the judges found a means of manipulating the law;
Article 376 of the civil code established that the father could
exercise his right of punishment if he had 'grave reasons for
discontent' with his child. It was the veracity of these reasons

for discontent and the degree of their gravity that the judges were henceforth to control by establishing a system of investigation that was to have a great future: the social enquiry. The petitioning father now himself became the object of an enquiry, in other words a suspect. The judiciary began to widen the field of its interventions, and its enquiries were not for long confined to the verification of a 'grave reason for discontent' between the father and his child. In 1890, questionnaires were printed for the use of the police and 'visiting nurses'. These recorded detailed information on the father and mother; profession, income(s), matrimonial status, information collected in the neighbourhood and from employers on the conduct and morality of the parents, their attitudes towards the child (later to be termed their 'educative capacities'), and finally a list of 'the unfortunate influences to which they might be subject'. It was, of course, the period for improving the labouring classes; Renouard[6] declared at the Academy of Moral and Political Sciences that 'the kind of order envisaged by the law is to be imposed upon ideas, habits, religious practices, morals and economics'. Jules Simon, president of many philanthropic societies who in 1876 had written a book against work for women[7], became the parliamentary apostle of a policy of healthy housing for workers, which advanced employers, at Mulhouse for example, began to apply on a grand scale: 'For the reform of workers' housing there is something else to do besides building houses, and that is to knock them down.'[8] In 1874, the Academy of Moral and Political Sciences announced an essay competition on the theme of 'The weekly day of rest from the point of view of morality, intellectual culture and industrial progress'. The winning entry, by a Parisian lawyer by the name of Joseph Lefort, saw in the Sabbath the means of 'revitalising family life', praised houses in the country, and the 'cabanons' (chalets) of the South, celebrated gardening, and appealed to employers to provide public lecture rooms. But he also emphasised the need to oppose corporate amusements, 'customs like those of the carpenters, which consist of organising a feast when a task is completed', and he proposed that French taverns should keep the hours of British pubs.[9]

Housing, work, leisure; these were the watchwords in the State's policing of production. The evolution of the practice and law of paternal punishment was also affected by this determination to eradicate diversity and 'savagery' from the social fabric. The 'panoptic and pangraphic' system of which Foucault speaks[10] presupposed a social transparency, the State's penetration into private life, by supervision, inquisition or denunciation. Hence the idea of substituting 'means of reform' for punishment, in the matter of working-class education. The fact was that, in reality, the desired reform was not aimed simply at the child – far from it. It was to embrace the whole family, even, if possible, the whole environment. The removal of the children was a means of penetrating and exerting pressure upon those families whose life had to change. Thus, on the subject of housing:

We have in Paris an Advisory Board of Insanitary Housing which does excellent work. It goes to visit the houses, and makes a report in which it states ... that instead of three inhabitants per room there were ten. Morality has disappeared. The whole family lives in the most deplorable promiscuity. The report reaches the Council, passes through the official channels and, finally, it takes about three years to succeed in evicting a householder from his house and during this time three generations of children are lost.[11]

On the subject of rest, which can only have meaning by reference to work and the factory:

the advantage of a day of rest on Sunday is that ... the peasant can educate himself by reading, the workman can give thought to his tools and try to improve them, the craftsman jeweller can go to museums.

And elsewhere we find statements such as the following:

it would appear to us proper that, in each factory, the employer should consent to become the moral instructor of his employees ... He would gain by this, because, instead of becoming orators, pronouncing words the sense and implications of which they sometimes fail to comprehend, his employees would remain honest craftsmen, interested in maintaining the established order of things.[12]

In the face of social diversity, it was necessary to decide upon a uniform compromise and impose it: the child was one means of doing so. Its temporary or permanent removal, or the threat of its removal, was a weapon the State and the philanthropic societies could use to impose their morality. The history of paternal punishment shows that two objectives were at stake: it was not a matter of educating children left running wild, as was the case for Doctor Itard,[13] but of replacing the practical and individual education provided by the child's environment with an education which was uniform, sophisticated, universal and geared to the production process. But at the same time, the aim was also to turn the family into a stereotyped unit, one that could consequently be regulated and disciplined. Through the social enquiry, that manifestation of the State's appropriation of the power of policing families (or, more elegantly put, of their power of self-regulation), a whole system for regulating families was introduced. Moreover, even as the family was being regulated, the further repression of vagrancy – followed by new legislation – made it even more impossible for children to run away.

A Marseilles lawyer describes the examination of a request for parental punishment at the end of the last century as follows:

The public prosecutor's office received the request and sent a questionnaire to be filled in to the organisation of visiting nurses for the French and for Italians domiciled in France ... Through the intermediary of highly dedicated and experienced assistants this organisation drew up a detailed and exhaustive record of particulars on the father, child and whole family. This record was returned, in duplicate, to the public prosecutor's office. One copy was sent to a specialist doctor ... A medical card was prepared, to which any other useful particulars, especially of a psychological nature, were appended. The second copy was sent to the office of vocational guidance, which was also in possession of a complete curriculum vitae of the minor, to be examined if necessary. These two bodies then submitted their own reports together with the information sent to them. The public prosecutor finally put the whole dossier together and, having listened to the father, drew up his own proposals. He passed all this information on to the presiding judge, who then pronounced judgement.

It was an altogether circular procedure. The National Assistance played a considerable role in the intensification of the use of the social enquiry, of re-educational confinement of indeterminate length and in subjecting families to pressures to conform, all of which culminated in the laws of 1904, 1908 and 1912. A member of its upper council, Brueyre, reported in 1899 to the General Society of Prisons (another breeding ground for social reformers):

Paternal correction is, in practice, an absolutely useless system, nothing but a form of punishment, which furthermore, because of the shortness of its duration, has absolutely no effect upon the child's re-education ... It should therefore be reformed and, to that end, one must have resort to the indeterminate sentence. After all, given that it is no longer a question of prescribing a punishment but rather of reconstructing a moral education, it is inconceivable that at the moment of pronouncing sentence, the judge should be able to estimate how long it should last for the education to produce useful results.[14]

In the course of the same meeting Professor Garçon gave his own definition of what was at stake in the above proposal:

I would like to protest against a number of theories which I find absolutely subversive to the idea of the family ... Certain men, assuredly motivated by the best intentions, but who are led utterly astray by their wish to do good, want to deprive the father of the family of the right to choose the establishment where he will have his son educated ... or to remove his child and switch to educating him in another establishment or in the family ... and when a child has been entrusted to their care, they even have the incredible pretension to keep him for as long as they please.[15]

The National Assistance did in fact have the power to act as guardian to 'morally abandoned children whose parents have been judged negligent in their duties'. The laws of 24 July 1889 and 19 April 1898 gave it powers to organise the dispossession of certain rights attached to paternal power, in particular the right of custody where the parents were 'unworthy or wretched'. In reality,

administrative practice had preceded legislation: the Conseil Général de la Seine had procured from parents of children whom it intended to withdraw from their guardianship, an undertaking to renounce their parental right in favour of National Assistance, or to reimburse the costs of education if they reclaimed their children before their age of majority.[16]

But the new legislation now made two decisive points official: the moral abandonment of the child could be a presumption, not a fact, and it could be presumed on the basis not of the child's conduct – 'which might well be beyond reproach'[17] – but on that of the parents. National Assistance and the numerous committees devoted to unhappy, irregular or delinquent children could thus operate through two procedures: first, through the investigations of their visiting nurses through denunciations made by local worthies, clergymen, employers or neighbours; and secondly through the undermining of the system of paternal punishment. Following the law of 1889, any father demanding a measure of paternal punishment might, by the end of the social investigation of his family, find the use of his right of punishment turned against him and, at the request of the National Assistance or of a committee, be deprived of the custody of his children. Take the Society for the Saving of Children: this was founded in 1867 by Pauline Kergomard (the crusader for nursery schools) and presided over by the inevitable Jules Simon. It became a public service in 1894. It, and societies like it, aimed to '*report* to the appropriate authorities and take in all children being ill-treated or in moral danger'. Children taken into care were placed in families 'in moderately easy circumstances', never more than one at a time. After thirteen years of age, they were apprenticed to farmers or craftsmen. Their contract stipulated that their wages be divided into five parts: one-fifth for pocket money, two-fifths for clothing and two-fifths placed with the savings bank. All visits or correspondence with the 'natural' family were forbidden. The girls were provided with a dowry by the Society.[18]

To promote families' morals and civilise their children, the National Assistance and the committees acted in the guise of orphanages. Paternal powers should henceforth be considered delegated by the State; the role of the family was to observe the rules of public hygiene and direct its offspring into the frameworks devised for them. In 1935, the law set its seal upon this manipulation of the *patria potestas*, by ruling that the presiding judge of the court should decide upon the duration of a placement requested through the channels of paternal punishment. Then, in the wake of the post-war reforms, the decree of 23 December 1958 quite simply abolished the right of paternal punishment, but granted the children's magistrate the right to appropriate it himself if 'the health, safety or morals of a minor are in danger'. Finally, the law of 4 June 1970, which reformulated Heading IX of the Civil Code as 'On Parental Authority', defined that authority as a function: 'a set of rights and duties *conferred upon* parents in the interest of the child, to ensure its protection and development'.

Meanwhile the legal machinery was redeployed and its role redefined. The only meaning of the notion of the child 'at risk' is that given it in practice by the policemen or social workers who are responsible for drawing attention to the bulk of the cases, or by the children's magistrates who deem it their duty to impose their authority. Establishing the criteria of intervention is entirely the province of the State machinery which is also the sole source of criteria for social mores, education, health and security. It follows therefore that all those subject to the jurisdiction of this protective justice will, whether adults or minors, be presumed irresponsible. This protective justice thus dispenses with a constant principle of French law, the principle of authority of the *res judicata*: the children's magistrate can by his own authority at any moment retract or modify his own decisions on the grounds of the obedience or the rebellion of the families and children in question.

Imprisonment loses its value at the point where the family becomes the ultimate satellite of the State; it is replaced by the AEMO, the function of which is simultaneously to intimidate, to improve, to tame and to model the family. This then is the reign of the social enquiry, of medico-psychological expertise, of powers of guardianship over a family's economic behaviour wielded by the authorities of social welfare until such time as the family be subdued or dislocated. The State's 'cleaning-up' operation is one of its principal activities and also one of the most covert. The social body is, to use Paul Virilio's expression, the 'final substance' on which the disciplinary power of the State is deployed.[19] Justice is protection (just as, in *Nineteen eighty-four*, 'war is peace'); health is protection (as, in *Nineteen eighty-four*, 'freedom is slavery').[20]

This protection – this protectorate – is inevitably accompanied by a rationale to counter every objection. Justification by production, justification by safety, justification by hygiene and by the Oedipus complex. The social body and its imaginative life are now compelled to be regularly domiciled. Adventure and surprise are banished, and the protected citizen is deemed to know nothing of himself or of any source of possible arguments against the system. Now the drama of Antigone is lived in reverse: interpretations take precedence over facts and twist them as they will, and the Sphinx-State, both ogre and omen, holds the key to that interpretation.

4

IRREGULAR CHILDREN AND THE POLICING OF FAMILIES

A man who doesn't like children can't be all bad.   (W. C. Fields)

The State's labour of atomising society has broken down complicated tribal structures into families, transforming a mass of multiple possibilities into an archipelago of egocentric little islands, and picking out and magnifying one essential figure: the child. The son or daughter 'of good family', is an infant monarch, whose every move is watched, whose every word is treasured, upon whom all the family's hopes are concentrated since he or she has absorbed almost all its energy. The vulnerable child, a recurrent literary theme although not one invariably chosen for the purest of motives, the mysterious child, inhabitant of another planet, a little prince whose lips pronounce the truth, the angelic child, the provisional repository of all that is best in humanity – even in books, eating children has not been allowed for a long time. The process leading to the family becoming the focal point of society has resulted in the construction of the positive stereotype of the child-god, upon whom the qualities of fragility, complexity and mystery have been progressively imposed. Meanwhile in contrast, it has labelled as irregular any family in which the offspring are not the gravitational centre. The child thus becomes a symptom, a pretext, a hostage, the currency of exchange in the operations of rehabilitation and re-education upon which various institutions are engaged. The atomisation of society into families has coincided with the appearance of the idea of childhood seen as a problem and the emergence of the concept of the 'maladjusted' child whose irregular characteristics fall into a special category constantly subject to subtle redefinition by the State apparatus.

In 1850, the law, which was beginning to sanction the actions of socialist prison experts such as Lucas and Demetz, and the power of statesmen such as the Baron de Gérando, who supported them,[1] made provision first for special prison quarters reserved for juvenile delinquents, then for reform schools wholly designed for taking delinquent minors into care. It is here, during the second half of the nineteenth century, that the idea of replacing imprisonment by re-education became established, and the practice of placing minors in institutions for an indeterminate time took over from that of depriving them of their liberty for a fixed period.

As the judicial apparatus was ceasing to be purely repressive, or at least purely incarceratory (although one should harbour no illusions as to the nature of these reformatories: they were farms where one worked hard, under military discipline) it was also moving towards a policy of 'supervisory education', that is to say towards the supervision of education in working-class families. By resisting the placing of their children for an indeterminate period of time for emotional reasons (separation), or economic ones (the loss of an income) or by way of a spontaneous reaction (to maintain their own particular traditions), families found themselves once again liable to judicial intervention: by setting themselves in opposition to the benefits of public action, they became the objects of suspicion and appraisal and the magistrates and authorities now considered their disinclination to cooperate to be one of the causes of the misfortunes of their offspring.

While penal placing was forced upon families against their wills, civil placing, of which they had been making use at their convenience, was little by little withdrawn from them. The right of parental correction, pared down by the courts, became the object of a barter: the father could still have his child confined, but only if he entrusted the child's upbringing to those more competent than himself and acknowledged his own incapacity.

For the children, in whose name this reform had been carried out, 'in order to spare them submission to the despotism of *patria potestas*', it meant not so much liberation from guardianship, as transition from one guardian to another.

In the last quarter of the century, the laws on the 'protection of ill-treated children' and on 'violence and assault and battery towards children', however generous their intentions, culminated in practices increasingly dependent upon the inspection – and hence the standardisation – of working-class education. The fact that there were battered children in some working-class families was used to justify the inspection of all working-class families to make sure their children were not battered. From the last quarter of the nineteenth century onwards, in criminal as in civil law, education became the central point of legal action.

The substitution of an agency for the control of families and the re-education of delinquents, in place of the notion of immediate chastisement for a definite fault, was accompanied by a technical modification of some importance: the transition from the notion of 'the extenuating excuse of minority' to that of 'irresponsibility'. Excused by his tender years, the minor was punished, but punished less. 'Irresponsible', he is not punished at all. He is 'taken into care'. This irresponsibility made it necessary to set up a special institution of adjudication – the children's court. At its creation in 1912, this was at first no more than an ordinary court of correction which sat in camera, making the justice of minors a justice of secrecy.

But stripping the delinquent of responsibility means not only surveillance of his family and his environment, but also that his offences are no longer punishable. I have already mentioned that after 1935 vagrancy was no longer considered a crime and called for no more than a measure of protection, that is to say control over the environment. It was a trend which ascribed less and less importance to the offence and more and more to the offender and his surroundings, and it was ratified by the ruling on the juvenile delinquent of 2 February 1945.

This document makes the irresponsibility of minors a maxim. It is a 'general and unconditional principal, without reference to any notion of discernment and regardless of the nature and gravity of the offence'.[2] The sentence becomes the exception; the minor can henceforth only be an object of measures of protection, education or reform. Jurisdiction for children becomes a truly specialised field, with its own particular procedures which allow the judge to review his decisions as often as he considers necessary, reducing or increasing their severity even when no further offences have been committed. Once the field becomes a specialised one, people who are not magistrates or even legally qualified are officially admitted into judicial procedures. The magistrates' advisors are chosen from among people who are known for 'the interest they take in questions concerning young people'. These are former members of the legal profession now retired, solicitors, notaries, barristers, policemen, the leaders of local industry, fathers or mothers of families whose numerous children or whose membership of some movement (parent–teacher association, scouts, cultural associations etc.) guarantee their positive allegiance to the idea that there is no alternative to the family for the well-being of the child, or doctors or social workers who are most commonly associated with the work of rehabilitating families. In addition, the children's magistrate receives the power to confiscate that part of the family income set aside by the State for children, namely the family allowance, and have it managed by specialists.

Jurisdiction for children now also officially introduced into judicial practice the taking into account of the minor's antecedents, personality and family, in other words, his environment. 'In all honesty', writes Paul Lutz, High Magistrate and future director of approved schools, 'the facts are here more important than the law.' It is the evaluation of the child and his environment which should, in effect, lay the foundations of the judge's decision. He must undertake an extensive enquiry on the minor's account, notably into his economic and moral situation and that of his family, the child's character and antecedents, his school attendance and attitude to school, the conditions under which he has lived and been raised. And, similarly, 'the social enquiry should be completed by a medical and medico-psychological examination, since it has been established that 80 per cent of delinquent children are ill or abnormal, physically or mentally deficient'.[3]

Based on the policies adopted with regard to families, a comprehensive body of laws for children was produced in 1958 and revised in 1970. The probation system became the 'keystone of penal legislation for children for it is through this that the children's magistrate retains a close and continuous control over the situation of minors, and since it makes it possible for him to review his original decision at any moment either to reduce or to increase its severity, to take account of the child's conduct'.[4]

Where civil legislation is concerned, it is the AEMO which provides the decisive inspiration for the new rulings. The purpose of this organisation is to 'aid and counsel the family' but it may give top priority to 'special obligations, such as regular attendance at a medical or educational establishment, or employment in some professional activity'.[5] As with the decisions of the probation system, the measures of AEMO may be 'at any moment modified or reviewed by the magistrate'.

Delinquent minors, pre-delinquents, physically or morally abandoned children, victimised children, all belong to the same family; they are all irregular and maladjusted. Whatever legal category they fall into, their irregularity stems from the same causes (family inadequacy, environmental influences, heredity) and manifests itself in the same ways (physical, intellectual or mental deficiency, behavioural problems, backwardness) ... whether or not they have actually committed an offence, the nature of these children is the same, they are amenable to the same remedies. That is the real problem so far as irregular children are concerned.[6]

State institutions responsible for surveillance, such as the police or the *gendarmerie*, or those whose purpose it is to establish a sort of leonine convention (such as providing services, like national insurance benefits, in exchange for the recipient's observance of a strictly determined line of behaviour) provide the framework for the care of these 'irregular children'. Within this framework, the children's magistrates organise the taking into care of families which evade surveillance or which break the contract. They take over all the functions formerly divided between the charitable organisations, the courts, the forces of law and order etc. Medicopsychological analysis, systematically used since 1945, provides a rationale for the strategy and methods of breaking down society into families and eliminating persistent rebels.

The demands of urbanism, of the economy, and of morality have been assembled to produce a State code the precepts of which define the tolerable limits of human behaviour. A century and a half after the first fruits of industrialisation, who can survive outside the framework – or free from the obsession – of the family?

A detailed and – in this instance – contemporary study of the social work of the State and its constant efforts to do away with the plurality of different ways of life, may make it possible to appreciate the shortsightedness and artificiality of the promotion of family isolation. Unaffected by utilitarian sociological motivation, a layman's impartial view of the archives and practices of the law courts and the services with which they collaborate, may discover the day-by-day triviality of this process of destruction.

In the France of the 1970s the distribution of family-making institutions was somewhat uneven: the industrial region of the North was where institutions connected with approved schooling were most numerous. The Court of Appeal of Douai was the second most active, after that of Paris, in terms of the number of civil and criminal cases involving minors brought before it. Breaking away from the over-dramatisation which generally prevails, wherever children and children 'with special problems' are concerned, the following study of the catchment area of Douai, originally part of a monograph, gives a detailed appraisal of the space for living that is left alongside the public space, of the extent to which officially acceptable behaviour is *de rigueur*, and of the methods adopted by the State to force families to lead a properly domiciled life.

Work on the monograph was carried out in 1973-4 in the catchment area of the Court of Douai. Apart from direct observation of juvenile courts and of the social medico-psychological services involved, it required a study of the legal files which record not only the judges' decisions but also all the documents relating to the open part of the procedure: the social enquiry, the specialists' opinions, consultations, and records of evidence of the police and *gendarmerie*. The law forbids the publication of the names of minors who appear before juvenile courts. The names we have used are fictitious. The texts between inverted commas are all extracts from the files. This research project was financed by the CORDES organisation.

INDIVIDUAL CASES OF DESTRUCTION

What the civil and criminal branches of justice for minors have in common is a policy of investigation into and intervention in the environment. But each has its own particular methods for apprehending those members of the population who fall under their jurisdiction. The justice of 'protection' proceeds by way of cooperation between the court, the institutions which are attached to it (the police, the social services ...) and those (the town hall, the school ...) which are in the position to supervise, control or provide information, in a direct and permanent manner on those who fall within the field of this jurisdiction. It can also be set in motion following a request for intervention emanating from a private individual, whether or not upon the advice of a representative of one of these institutions.

Criminal justice functions by means of a simple technique; the department of public prosecutions lays charges against a minor arrested by the police and accused of an offence. Apart from this difference of 'seizure', civil law and criminal law use the same methods and, frequently even the same people: social enquiries, psychological and psychiatric examinations, observation, orientation, etc. While they resemble each other in principle these measures are the responsibility of different services: the probation services for the delinquent, AEMO for children 'at risk'. But the children are all placed in the same boarding schools or homes, and it is only placement in prison, with or without remission, that is reserved exclusively for juvenile delinquents. Delinquents can furthermore be sentenced either by the children's magistrate alone, in a closed court, or in a magistrates' court, in the presence of two assessors and the prosecutor of the Republic, while 'minors at risk' are only heard and 'protected' in 'closed court'.

Bearing these differences in mind, it is possible to describe and analyse the jurisdiction of minors and the institutions attached to it, considering criminal law and the civil law together, and indicating where apropriate any features that are peculiar to the one or the other.

THE OFFENCE AS A PRETEXT

The offences which are at the origin of the actions before the children's court almost all fall into three simple categories:

The stealing of means of locomotion is, nearly always, a borrowing of a moped in order to return home one day when the journey on foot or on a bus seems impossible, of a car to go on a spree with mates to get away from the sober charms of Roubaix-Tourcoing for a while, or to show one knows how to drive, or to 'break out' from a centre or from home, or even to drive it 200 metres and then abandon it, just a matter of killing boredom. The motor is almost always found again a little later, in the town where it was taken, perhaps in the same place and, in any case, never further away than the amount of petrol in the tank can take it. Of 140 sentences on minors passed by the children's magistrate in January 1970 at Lille, thirty-seven were for stealing a car, a lightweight motorbike or a bicycle.

The arrest may take place in the course of a traffic control or by a caretaker or by the owner – who usually takes the thief to the police station as soon as possible – or perhaps he is led to own up in the course of an interrogation, after being arrested

for another matter. Thus young Davergne (17 years old, from a
family of four children which lives on the salary of one of the
sisters who is a machine winder on 850 francs per month[7]), was
arrested in November 1969 for the theft of a handbag, and
while he was in custody admitted the theft of sixty-seven cars
between September 1968 and January 1969. 'Sometimes we
pinched five or six cars in the same night. We drove around for
a bit and then left them.' The police, as is customary, on the
off-chance, read him their list of car thefts for which the thieves
had never been caught and 'under interrogation', to use the
police jargon, they got him to remember, eleven months after
the presumed actions, the sixty-seven thefts, by giving him the
number, the make and the colour of each car, and the date and
place of the thefts. This feat of memory earned Davergne
fifteen months in prison, without any further proof. Sometimes
at the hearing of the juvenile court the boy who, in circumstances such as these, has been his own accuser, explains that
he was under duress. Physical force would not always be
necessary and several hours of custody, two or three gestures of
intimidation, and the boy's ignorance of his rights would be
enough to make him sign anything 'to be cleared'.

One can also be denounced by a mate or by one's parents or
even, in the case of Christian Verschave, steal from a school
playground the bicycle of a policeman, who thereupon con-
ducts his own enquiry in the *quartier*, finds his bicycle, makes his
complaint and demands that Christian's father, in whose
garage the bike was stored, be accused of concealing stolen
goods.

The theft of goods, which constitutes the second category of
offences checked by the children's court and magistrate is,
nearly always, shop-lifting in large stores and supermarkets. Of
the 140 minors who appeared in court in Lille in January 1970,
sixty were there for this reason. It is the cashiers of these
establishments or, more often, the store detectives whom they
employ, who instigate the arrest. Of the sixty boys and girls up
for judgement in January 1970, none had stolen merchandise
of a value greater than 163.80 francs. The big stores, which

recovered the merchandise, nevertheless brought charges and demanded damages which the court furthermore granted them. Thus the manager of a big store in Roubaix declared, after having handed over Curdia Abdelkader to the police, 'One of my salesgirls having remarked the dubious conduct of a young Algerian girl drew my attention to it and I had her searched. I had been robbed of goods to the value of 6.35 francs and I am bringing charges.' Curdia (16 years old, oldest of a family of seven with the father absent, and living on 986.15 francs of family allowances) had stolen a pair of scissors (value 4.50 francs) and a box of pins (value 1.85 francs).

The list of thefts judged in January 1970 gives an idea of the activity of children's magistrates and juvenile courts:

1 clockwork bird
1 notebook
2 penknives
1 packet of screws
1 battery
1 putty knife
2 bars of chocolate
2 packets of sweets
1 eggtimer
1 airgun
1 dart
2 packets of razor blades
2 pencil sharpeners
1 packet of coffee
1 bottle of wine
1 pot of jam
1 gas lighter
1 hammer

1 mascara
1 bottle of nail varnish
1 lipstick
1 ring

1 blouse

3 packets of biscuits
1 loaf
sausages
1 butcher's knife
1 pair of scissors
1 box of pins
1 packet of nuts
1 child's dress
1 little bottle of Roja-Plis Belle colour
1 bottle of Coca-Cola
2 packets of chewing gum
2 litres of soda water

1 brooch
1 fishing rod
1 tin of sausages
2 penholders
1 artificial flower
2 fishing lines and 3 floats
1 box of shirt-sleeve buttons
1 record
1 penknife

1 alarm clock
biscuits
1 handkerchief
sweets

1 bottle of nail varnish
1 roll of adhesive tape

1 Kelton watch
smoking equipment
2 red sweaters
1 pair of Mitonfle tights

1 pair of socks
1 set of children's handkerchiefs
2 green bathing costumes
2 pairs of bathing trunks

3 packets of cigarettes
1 packet of pastry
1 film

1 blouse
1 Ricils pencil

1 pullover
1 pair of sunglasses
3 rings
1 transistor

6 cans of cat food
2 packets of sweets
1 packet of biscuits
1 bottle of rum
1 pot of yogurt
1 musical box

1 record
2 pairs of shoes

tit-bits

cigarette lighters

1 scarf
1 comb

2 pairs of socks
3 cigarette lighters

tit-bits
toys

2 pairs of gloves
transfers

Apart from shop-lifting, the magistrate and juvenile court
were concerned with thefts of handbags (six/140), thefts from
caravans (one umbrella and one mac), from building sites
(20kg of copper), of money (125 francs, 26 francs from jackets,
80 francs from a purse, 40 and 300 francs, 12 and 40 francs
from purses, etc.), from holiday homes (200 francs worth of
various objects, ranging from a weaver's glass to a wood chisel,
a fishing rod, etc.). Two boys of 11 and 13 years even found
themselves in closed court for having 'defaced movable objects
belonging to a third party, namely: a Berliet lorry, a cement
mixer, a concrete mixer, a compressor and a bulldozer' which
placed them under probation until they reached the age of 20.

Next after thefts of means of locomotion and of merchandise,
comes the third category of offences, much more infrequent,
namely, outrages to public decency (five/140). Except in the
rare cases in which there is a flagrant offence (René B. who
'followed the woman P. in the street and put his hand up her
skirts' and was arrested and taken to the station by a witness),
it is usually the parents of the young girl who make the
complaint. The procedure which follows the complaint is quite
complicated: sometimes the boy and girl say there was mutual
consent, and they are found guilty of outraging public decency,
since, in most cases they made love 'in a place visible to all',
that is to say elsewhere than in the parents' home, in a place
where third parties would have been able to see them. They
are, in fact, seen as it were retrospectively, by means of a legal
contrivance. This is what happened to Martine P. ($17\frac{1}{2}$ years
old, eldest of three, father pensioned on 1,350 francs a quarter,
herself a worker on 650 francs a month) and Carlo D. ($17\frac{1}{2}$
years old, father on the dole, fourth of seven children and a
carpet layer at 700 francs a month). Martine secretly took

money out of her wages to give it to Carlo or spend it with him. Her father noticed, and Martine fell into a panic and said that Carlo had forced her to sleep with him and had extracted money from her. The father made a complaint and during her interrogation Martine retracted, saying that she had consented. However, as she declared that she and Carlo had made love in the open air and therefore in a 'place visible to all' they were both judged and sentenced for an outrage to public decency. In other cases, the young girl, fearing she is pregnant, or being so, tells her parents, who persuade her to say that she had not consented and make a complaint. Indictments for rape – which involve an appearance before the court of assizes – are not often upheld by the public prosecutor's office, and the young man is tried for a criminal offence to morals, which brings him at the minimum a suspended sentence and quite frequently a prison sentence.

After these three major categories, indictments for causing bodily harm and offences of the fifth category – namely former misdemeanours now considered criminal by the law – make up the remainder of the cases that come before the juvenile magistrate and court, not counting 'incidents during probation' which I shall discuss at the same time as that measure. We might also mention a number of examples which, although unusual, are nevertheless worthy of attention, such as that of Nadine Allaert, sentenced for infringement to railway regulations because she travelled first-class with a second-class ticket in order to return on time to the detention centre where she had been placed by a previous decision; or that of Franco Zanetti, placed in a detention centre for carrying a weapon of the sixth degree, in other words a clasp-knife with a lock-back.

The most obvious characteristics of criminal justice for minors are the homogeneity of the social origin of the delinquents, the petty nature of the offences for which they are brought to trial, the high proportion of large families among those affected by the jurisdiction of minors, the low standard of their housing and the low level of their incomes. While stealing – borrowing a car or moped appears both as a way of momentarily enjoying something one cannot oneself afford, of getting away, just for a while, from the family and the *quartier* and enjoying a little adventure and distraction, the shop-lifting is on the other hand almost always utilitarian and relates directly to the economic situation of these families: what are stolen are clothes, food and toys. It would be almost embarrassing to make such obvious points were it not for the fact that all the official reports that the police, the judiciary and its assistants, and the specialists produce on such cases begin by ignoring and end up by denying them.

But the homogeneity of the social origin of convicted minors, and likewise the pettiness of the offences committed by them, both betray the existence of a systematic desire to control a particular section of the population, and the fact that the offence is simply used as a pretext to intervene. What is the nature of this control? And, having determined which section of the population it is aimed at and one of the procedures for reaching it, can one also determine what these people are being censured for and what it is that juvenile justice is seeking to control? The social enquiry, a method common to both criminal and civil law, makes it possible for us to discover what it is that juvenile justice is tracking down in the working-class family.

FAMILIES UNDER INSPECTION

Nothing can compare with the enigmas of the protocol applied to humble folk.   (Raymond Radiguet)

In accordance with the judicial machinery, the social enquiry may be carried out either by the police or *gendarmerie*, or by a social service (and sometimes the latter duplicates the work of the former) but in either case the same methods are used and the same facts investigated. The communication addressed by the magistrate to the police or the *gendarmerie* when making his request for an enquiry provides an interesting record. This document is composed of six sections concerning the family and six concerning the minor: *composition of the family* (civil status of the children, to be checked on the appropriate documents: indicate whether legitimate, illegitimate, adopted, legitimised ...); *habitat* (mother's management: bad, average, good; isolated rural, non-isolated rural, working class, bourgeois, residential, or mixed area; *type of habitation* (council house, housing estate, *pension* or hotel or suitable lodgings, dubious hotel or café ...); *resources, hygiene* (do they have medical attention when necessary? is there a family doctor? composition of meals ...); *family history* (contacts with the investigator, résumé of the family's past, who exercises the dominant influence in the household? previous convictions; social services involved with the family ...); *personality of parents* (character: egoistical, vain, ambitious, sincere, quarrelsome, gambling, conduct and morality; educational capacity, work ...). As to the minor, the six points of investigation are: *personal record* (pregnancy, normal or difficult birth; religion – practising? previous convictions ...) *school attendance* (regularity, results); *activity or profession* (stability, ability, opinion of employer); *health* (at what age did he stop being incontinent? anything specially remarkable on the sexual front?); *behaviour* (unambitious or dynamic, reflective or impulsive, has he played truant, even for a short time? bossy or obedient without argument? sociable or withdrawn); *leisure* (family amusements, staying out late, dances and flirtations, cafés, cinema visits, pocket money ...). The completed memorandum should be followed by the investigators reasoned conclusions as to what steps should be taken.

So the object is to verify a certain number of points connected with the traditional criteria of public morality: notably that the minor and his family demonstrate total allegiance to the fundamental institutions. The couple must be legitimate, likewise the children, the house must be respectably run and by the mother, the doctor called at the right moment, the dominant influence must be exercised by the husband, the father, who must be stable and conscientious in his work, religion must be seen to be respected in the observance of one

or two rites at least such as baptism and communion, attendance at school or work must be regular and zealous, and
amusements, such as television, found within the family and
home.

But it is also a matter of identifying all the more or less
atypical or non-conformist aspects in the family way of life; the
home should not be too isolated, dubious, or shared with
others, manifesting neither a suspect unsociability nor a sociability which gives the environment a quality difficult to define.
Sometimes it is considered that the 'family atmosphere is not
good, because the couple moves house many times in unfash-
ionable *quartiers* where they live alongside North Africans,
tramps, and other people from socially undesirable environ-
ments', or that 'as in most families resident in the populous city
of T., the family climate does not inspire confidence'. Acceptable housing, in contrast, will be 'situated in a housing estate
for miners' or in a 'well situated and adequately lit housing
estate'. The habitat must be accessible to supervision and
organised in such a way that neighbours are clearly separated
from one another and there is none of the overcrowding that
breeds brawling and crime.

Whatever its location within the urban fabric, the home
must conform to well-defined rules of hygiene and organisation. It must be sufficiently furnished: 'in a manner neither
summary nor odd'. It may nevertheless be acceptable for it to
be 'without style, but not too sparsely furnished', or even
'scantily furnished' if it is 'in the Arab style'. Particular
disapproval is incurred by several children sleeping in the same
bed, whether this be for reasons of custom or economy. Just as
sharing housing with strangers to the family denotes a form of
capillary sociability considered to be exotic in the case of Arab
families, and archaic in that of French ones, children sharing a
bed is indicative of a dense mode of family life, and is thus
equally archaic and unsuitable. 'The four Tassigny girls sleep
head-to-tail in a single bed.'[8]

The question of the family's nutrition is scrutinised without
reference to the family resources: it is noted that the Ahmed

family, where there are eleven children and the widowed father earns 900 francs a month (in 1970) buy '10 francs of meat, four 1,200 gramme loaves, and 3 litres of milk every day'. In particular, it is noted that they have 'no reserve provisions' and that 'the marketing is done on a day-to-day basis'. Note is taken of whether 'the meals are abundant and satisfying' and whether the family appears capable of organising the way it eats and shops in a rational fashion.

These observations, without the slightest reference to the material situation of the families are used, together with others which I shall be examining presently, to determine whether the minor who is guilty of one of the offences listed above 'can be left in his family environment' and 'whether it is necessary to take any measures with regard to this environment' or to decide whether 'the health, morality, security and education' of a child are 'at risk'. Progressively they elaborate a model of social hygiene and, at the same time, indicate the degree of the judicial enquiry's penetration into these families. The task of the social enquiry is to determine whether the environment is stable, sterile and standard. It is standard if its mode of life is organised around a space which is functionalised and definitive and neither affected by chance nor adaptable: a habitat which is average and middle of the road, the furnishings indicating positive home 'planning', the rooms organised with a view to the furniture rather than the convenience of a swarm of children. Hygiene is taken to mean recourse to the medical establishment; nutrition, familiarity with a particular style of consumption.

The environment is sterile and stable when it is turned in upon itself, its contacts few and organised, aseptic. As the enquiries of the social investigation reveal, they are more concerned with the conduct and morality of parents than with discovering whether the social conventions are observed. It is not a question of registering the concrete material problems experienced by the families but rather their aberrations. It is with relief that, after a long chapter of pedagogic tribulations, the researcher can report on the Wallaerts, that 'the father has had his left leg amputated and is hemiplegic, the mother is paraplegic and has had her right kidney removed. In the past, the emotional relationship between the couple was not good. Now peace and calm reign once more; the father never leaves home, except by ambulance. His conduct and his morality no longer leave anything to be desired. Nor can fault be found with the mother from the point of view of conduct and morality. Since her paralysis, she is no longer as cantankerous as she used to be.'

Also stabilised are the Magniez, a common-law couple; he 'suffers from a varicose ulcer on the right leg, a stomach ulcer and a cardiac deficiency. Madame is swollen with elephantiasis and also suffers from a cardiac deficiency. They seem to live in perfect harmony. They do not drink. Nevertheless, their educational understanding is very limited.' Family peace must be like the peace of a cemetery.

Meanwhile, one can be a good man without being paraplegic or affected with elephantiasis: M.D. is a 'good worker, who seldom goes out and does not frequent cafés. His only leisure activity is cultivating his garden.' Mme F. on the other hand, leads a 'deplorable life, she often mixes with North Africans and goes to their cafés'. Mme K. 'entertains a succession of North Africans as limited as herself'; Mme G. 'consumes rather a lot of wine and beer in the company of dubious individuals, notably a rag-and-bone man and an Algerian'. Mme Z. 'has had numerous lovers, both Italians and North Africans' and 'does not seem to be in possession of all her mental faculties'.

While Mme H. 'is still in bed at 10 in the morning', Mme V. 'was doing her housework when we made contact with this family at 8.15'. Mme M. 'flighty and thriftless, neglects the household to frequent cafés with her husband'; Mme P. is 'holder of the *médaille de la famille française*'. Widowed at the age of 35 she has had eight children, now between 17 and 2 years old. They live in an F5 (a newly constructed type of *appartement* consisting of five rooms, excluding the kitchen and bathroom) on 1,728 francs a month, all told. M. X. 'has stayed at home without working and without being registered at a labour exchange despite the fact that he has been in perfectly good health, for three months'.

M. D., who 'is blind in one eye and has facial burns, likes to go on a binge and is led astray by his spouse, with whom he frequents cafés'. At the W. home by contrast, 'the indications are that there is no discord between the couple. Since purchasing a car, they go out on Sundays and watch television during the week.'

All movements and activity outside the framework established by the family, where they live and amuse themselves, and their place of work, is suspect and legitimate cause for legal intervention. It is not alcoholism that is harried, but the frequenting of cafés, particularly if the husband and wife go there together, for this is a sign that they are deserting their responsibilities, moving beyond the perimeter. If the real or imagined moral laxity of the mother attracts so very much disapproval, it is because she turns neighbourliness into promiscuity, so that it soon becomes difficult to tell who's who.

The social enquiries are also concerned to track down wandering and disorganisation in minors. Alain G. 'has no routine, he hangs around in cafés, has no worthwhile leisure activities, goes to the cinema five times a week showing absolutely no discrimination'. In addition 'he keeps his wages' (800 francs a month). The report concludes that for this boy, who has stolen a car, 'a strict regime is desirable'. Houssine M. is an undisciplined subject. 'In 1968 he was sometimes away from home for a fortnight at a time. He would regularly come home late, offering no explanation.' Alain D. 'frequented dances and cinemas and often came home late'. B. 'seems rather secretive; he goes out with mates and gets home rather late on Saturday; he seems to be trying to organise outings and drag along his mates'. As to Brahim D., 'he has left his father's house to go to live with a woman who is involved in a divorce case'.

All these boys are working, either in the factory or at CET (Technical College) but reveal, individually or with others, an eccentricity and an independence that bodes ill and is at odds

with the 'regularity' of those such as René Georges, who is
'very attached to his elder brother, is a member of a working-
class education club and would benefit from a degree of
clemency', or Jean M. who 'does not frequent cafés and
cinemas and consecrates a part of his free time to studying his
books', or Abdelhamid K. who 'spends part of his leisure time
learning to write Arabic' or Alain S. who 'likes reading and
educational games'.

Free time must be spent in a social, institutional manner;
reading and educational games help one to get on at school or
at work, the cinema five times a week is a sort of harmful
withdrawal from social life. The working-class educational
club or centre can welcome, direct and mould an appetite for
contacts, but nobody can keep an eye on the outings of a gang
which comes home late. So it is no surprise to find that Claude
Benoit is 'unconcerned when faced with an act which should,
in normal circumstances, affect him, such as the case of the
present enquiry'. He is not playing the game. The place to
have attachments is the family, the place to go out to is a youth
club, the place of work must be a regular one and, to mitigate
independence, money must be pocket-money.

But if the family does not submit to these rules, it must be
protected (the Spanish would say that it must be 'interfered
with'). Thus the Delatre family 'has the reputation of harbouring shady young people, some of whom it knows to be sought
by the police. A number of girls and boys have been observed
seeking shelter there. Yet, the place has nothing to attract
sensible people to stay there. There is no television in this
home, no means of amusement. Nevertheless, we have on
several occasions noticed Mme Delatre and her two sisters
dancing in the courtyard to the music of a transistor radio. At
all events, it would seem wise to intervene firmly in this
environment, which is disturbed by the bad conduct of the
mother, who shamelessly permits couples of idlers to get
together in her home, hold parties there and indulge in actions
which are an offence to morality.'

The family should not be a shelter, but a place of no secrets.

Action on the part of the AEMO, reinforced by a permanent threat to remove the five children, put an end to the dancing and to the unsuitable behaviour, and the Delatres will have to move house and pay their debt to urbanity.

The families which request the intervention of the children's magistrate are complaining of the same independence and carefree attitude: 'I have the honour of soliciting your attention in the matter of my daughter whose conduct is shocking. She keeps company with an Algerian man and spends whole nights away with him. She will accept no reprimand and is rough with my wife and me when we try to prevent her from going back to this man. I would like her to be placed before a misfortune occurs' (letter from M. Debat, a miner invalided by silicosis, on the subject of his daughter, Annie, 16 years). 'I request you to summons my daughter Christine who spends her time as she pleases, missing her lessons, accepting invitations to dine with adult men or youths' (letter from M. Belin, shopkeeper, about his 17-year-old daughter). 'I have the honour of bringing your attention to the question of the behaviour of my daughter Evelyne, aged 17 years. She is slipping further and further from my authority. For example, she left home on Saturday about 5 in the afternoon to go out for about half an hour, and has still not returned, two days later. I do not know when she will return, with whom she is, where she is or what she is doing' (letter from Mme Monet, municipal cook).

Then the social enquiry has its say: 'Annie was still in bed yesterday at 11.30 in the morning and showed little inclination to get up despite the entreaties of her mother who had told her of our presence. She was badly washed and excessively made-up, wearing paste rings on her fingers. Christine goes to the Pigier class at Maubeuge, which means she leaves early and comes back late (she lives in Valenciennes). At mid-day she eats in the cafés in the vicinity of the school. This excessive freedom has certainly not been of benefit to her.' As to Evelyne, she is 'lazy and unstable and has categorically refused to take communion'.

DR DIAFOIRUS TAKES A DEEP BREATH[9]

It is important to note that in criminal cases the children's magistrate acts as an examining magistrate,[10] but that, whereas in cases involving adults the examining magistrate's task is to shed light on the charges, that is, to investigate the offences and evidence; the children's magistrate, in his capacity as examining magistrate for minors, never concerns himself with the material facts. For these he relies entirely upon the police report. There are no grounds for making an artificial contrast between the criminal law for adults, which falls within the province of citizens' rights, and that of minors: the frequent use of the procedure known as 'direct summons'[11] ultimately results in similar situations. It is nonetheless interesting to note that children's justice officially sanctions and encourages the practice of collusion between the judicial apparatus and the police apparatus.

The children's magistrate examines the minor's personality and environment, rather than the facts of the case. The social enquiry is the first step in this 'examination', and, in so far as it is the first procedural action in affairs of minors 'at risk', it provides the first indication of the functions and methods of juvenile justice. However, to complete his investigation of the behaviour and lifestyle of those involved, the children's magistrate has other means at his disposal: he can order a period of provisional probation or supervision in an open environment, in the course of which the child and his family are studied at home during a variable time, generally between one and three months, by a social worker. Equally, he can order a 'personality study', this will be made by the vocational guidance consultative body (COE) and will include a psychological examination, a psychiatric examination and a 'synthesis' under the direction of an educational officer. Finally, he can order the provisional placement of the minor in an observation centre. This is a boarding institution, where the minor stays between three and five months, at the end of which an educational, psychological and psychiatric report, together with definite recommendations, is sent to the magistrate. All these measures, which may be taken separately, apply to civil as well as criminal law.

However, not all juvenile courts are backed up with the machinery necessary for them to make frequent use of such procedures. That of Valenciennes, for example, has no vocational guidance consultation organisation of its own. The trend is to make such machinery more generally available,[12] but it is meanwhile clear that, even where it exists, it cannot be used systematically for all the delinquent minors or minors at risk who come before the children's magistrate. It is thus interesting to discover which are the minors for whom the magistrate orders a 'personality study' or provisional placement in an observation centre, or psychiatric treatment. Despite the technical differences between these methods, a simultaneous analysis of their functioning and functions may be justified by their common relation to one of the central policies of justice for children, namely the introduction of medicine, psychology and pedagogy into judicial investigation and action.

In a number of marginal cases of little statistical importance, the magistrate uses vocational guidance consultation and the observation centre when the minor and the minor's family are uncooperative and withhold information in the course of the social enquiry, or when a provisional measure, such as observation in an open environment has been adopted. Thus, the probation officer responsible for a provisional measure taken in the case of Ahmed C. requests that he be examined at the vocational centre, because 'he is very close, and his relationship with the authorities is marked by reticence and dissimulation'. Similarly, the social worker responsible for the enquiry into François F. and his family asks that he should be placed in an observation centre because 'the parents have refused entry to their apartment, have been summoned twice and have not come, and I have not been able to have an interview alone with François except in my car'.

Apart from such marginal cases, the children's magistrate uses vocational guidance consultation and the observation centre for particularly rebellious minors and for those whose environment was not judged to be too unfavourable when it was the object of the social enquiry.

Of the children examined at the COE or at an observation centre (CO), 51 per cent are truants from the boarding schools or homes where they have been placed, either by the decision of a previous sentence, or by order of the local health and social authorities, or else by their families. Whether they are liable to penal or to 'protective' measures depends on whether or not they committed thefts of cars or motorbikes for a quick getaway, or of money or goods to feed or clothe themselves during their flight. Ten per cent are recidivists at playing truant and 8 per cent have run away from their families. That accounts for more than two-thirds of the minors examined in consultation or in the centre following refusals – generally repeated – to take up the place suggested for them by the placement centre, or school or their family, and for three-quarters if one adds those (4 per cent) who are examined at the request of their parents.

The rest are sent by the magistrate following thefts not committed while running away (23 per cent), generally thefts in a gang or thefts more serious than the average, or else for sexual matters, outrage to public decency, prostitution (4 per cent).

Thus consultation and the centre are used, in the majority of cases, when the investigation of the environment conducted by the social enquiry does not provide sufficient basis for an intervention. The fugitives may have been placed in a boarding school or a home because the family environment had previously been judged 'dangerous' by the social enquiry carried out by a juvenile court, or deficient by the department of health and social action and, in this case, the minor's running away indicates that the choice of placement was wrong, so other reasons to intervene must be found, and other modes of intervention. Alternatively, the minor may have been placed by the family, so clearly by an environment taking its 'educational' responsibilities seriously and in such a case the social enquiry would not find grounds for action. Or again, the minor may be in flight from his parental home and, in this case, and whatever may be the conclusions of the social enquiry, it would be illusory and literally utopian to hope that he could receive any degree 'of education with support from the environment' such as might be provided through probation or AEMO.

In the face of the resistance of boys and girls to being taken into institutional care and to the mode of life which the social enquiries commend, it becomes necessary to devise a new strategy and find new ways to justify the judicial institutions.

In addition, a measure of inadequacy and failure on the part of the social enquiry is indicated by the type of family of a good third of the minors taken into care through consultation and the centre. These are boys and girls, mostly sent there by the magistrate as the result of an offence rather than of a protection procedure, who come from an environment with which the social enquiry can hardly find fault: families of skilled workers, living in a clean apartment block in a newly developed area, some of them on the way to becoming home owners – families that are concerned that their children should not be 'left too much to their own devices' and that do not present any noticeably disordered characteristics.

But the child's thefts, or in some cases his running away, if repeated often enough, automatically imply legal intervention: the 'good' environment now plays a contradictory role: the juvenile court is disinclined to send to prison the son or daughter of a family which is, if not respectable, at least presentable, and favours an 'educational' placement. But an assessment of the family way of life does not support this justification: the health, the morality and the safety of the minor are in no more danger than his education. The inspection of the family's way of life does not provide sufficient justification for taking the child into care, so does not operate effectively. An intermediary procedure is needed. It is provided by consultation and the centre, for these offer a new set of criteria, make a new investigation possible, provide new standards to take over from those which the social enquiry has been bound to respect within the intimacy of the families, and widen the boundaries within which the legal investigation can operate.

These institutions have three methods for legitimising further legal intervention. The first is to suggest that the child is mentally defective in order to explain his behaviour; the second, to suggest he is retarded, by examining his Oedipus complex and the third, to devalue and blame his family through an analysis of the interrelations between its members. It goes without saying that these three methods can be combined.

SUGGESTING THAT THE CHILD IS DEFECTIVE

By and large, almost all the boys and girls examined through consultation and the boys observed in the centre, trail behind them a mild suggestion of defectiveness, because they have failed to attain the appropriate IQ level in the institutions' compulsory psycho-technical tests. The explanation and analysis of the actions and behaviour of all these minors are thus always seen against a background of mental weakness which serves to set the tone, and to legitimise medical treatment for the offence, in other words to legitimise intervention in the first place. But certain reports assign a place of particular importance to feeble-mindedness. They chiefly concern minors who are satisfied with the explanation which they themselves give for their actions. Thus, Christian Verschave has stolen a bicycle. The consultant-psychiatrist who examines him notes: 'when one asks him if he is good at his work, he replies, "Yes." When one then immediately asks him if he is bottom of the class, he replies, "Yes." Once he took a 50 franc note from the house and bought toys for himself and for his brothers. He has stolen a moped. He justifies his action as follows: "I didn't have one so I took one." This is a case of mental deficiency and emotional retardation prone to suggestibility and anxious for approval.' The synthesis of the consultation concludes that placement in a medico-professional institute is the appropriate treatment. Likewise Ali Larbi, 'when one broaches the subject of his offences with him, his responses are very stereotyped, of the type: "everyone's done silly things". He is a medium mental defective.' It was advised that he be placed in a Medico-Pedagogical Institute (IMP). Aline Trichaud, 'an adolescent with a lunatic appearance ... is a primitive being who is satisfied with being an object. (She is 17 years old and occasionally prostitutes herself.) An IMP would help her to develop.'

Coupled with the idea of debility, the notion of suggestibility is used to establish that the minor, victim of the bad company he keeps, has neither the intelligence nor the character to resist the harmful influences of his acquaintances: Michel Trembert, 'extremely immature, thinks only of amusing himself and fitting in with those around him (he has taken part in a gang theft of money). For this mentally deficient boy, so susceptible to influence and suggestion, it is urgent to break the cycle of bad influences and we think it necessary to have recourse to a placement in an educational home.' Alain Marie, who has taken part in a car theft on the occasion of a collective escape, 'is an unstable defective, suggestible and easily influenced, with too weak a personality to control his urges. He must be confined; given the proper framework his development may be favourable.'

Mental deficiency is also used to explain the behaviour of Jean-Pierre D., 15 years old, who has already made eight escapes, each one accompanied by the theft of a means of transport and of foodstuffs, and who 'is so concerned not to come out of the childhood world of play and dream, that he is incapable of emotional attachment. He is internally incoherent and in need of imposed rules and regularity.' A little further on, we provide the entire transcript[13] of a consultative psychiatric report for the vocational education authorities concerning 14 year old Claude X., who was arrested for stealing cash (250 francs). This is a typical report based on the method of classifying a child as defective.

EXAMINING THE OEDIPUS COMPLEX

The second method of legitimising intervention, given the minor's 'failure to recognise his guilt' consists in deducing from this an incapacity to control his own existence and in explaining this situation by a pathology of the Oedipal process.

Daniel G. (numerous escapes from an Aide Sociale à l'Enfance home, with thefts of motorbikes and other things) 'is an illegitimate child raised by his grandfather. The image of his father is very devalued. The boy interiorises the problem that stems from his paternity. The escapes represent his first reaction to this intolerable situation. He is of normal intelligence and spirited, but his potential is blocked by the emotional problem. When one tries to broach the subject of his future with him, he confesses that he does not think about it often. For him the future is now.'

Jacques D. (16 years old, placed in a home by legal decision) 'is so choosy about offers of employment that none will do for him. He never stays more than a few days in a job. He is capable of self-criticism but will not really accept any blame. He fears his father but does not love him; identification with him is totally negative. He has definite obsessional tendencies and an obvious failure complex. The Oedipal conflict has not been resolved. His incapacity to acclimatise to the factory where he has to work, and his block before assimilation are indicative of a phenomenon of obsession-compulsion, resulting in emotional traumas. This is a fragile and neurotic personality; the important thing is to encourage him gradually to come to terms with his conflicts and their origin.'

Daniel Quesnay has run away from a home and stolen things to live on. He is 19 years old 'his face is sad and old, he has the pale complexion of a boy who has no holidays. He has only his mother. The absence of any paternal reference is a deficiency which contributes to the bleak, dead, emotional climate. He has an inferiority complex which hinders him from taking part in social situations. One must help him to take his place in society by giving him confidence in himself.'

Michel Albert, 14 years old, is accused of stealing. His father is a total invalid. 'The behavioural problems which he manifests at the moment may be considered as an expression of the strong emotional needs of an adolescent whose conflictual family situation generates anxieties and prevents him from achieving interpersonal relations, except on an egocentric basis.'

Mireille Vercauten, 18 years old, has knowingly received 200 francs arising from a housebreaking and used it to buy a stone destined for the grave of her step-father; 'she shows absolutely no feelings of guilt and seems to have little moral sense. Her disturbances arise from a lack of instruction. All her relationships are superficial, without real involvement. They produce very little reaction on her part. Her characteristic personality traits are passivity and non-engagement; she has no real desires, experiences little anxiety. We do not see any point in undertaking lengthy measures in the case of this girl who is so little given to introspection; nevertheless, a probation order might be useful, as a warning.'

BLAMING AND DEVALUING THE ENVIRONMENT

The vocational education consultation and the observation centre establish two disqualifications, one for the minor and one for his environment. If not founded on a social enquiry, legal intervention, which will result in separating the one from the other, will stem from the consultation or the recommendations of the centre either on the grounds that the environment is too rejecting, or that it is overprotective. Rejection and overprotection, both considered to produce reactions of distress in the minor, explain his behaviour and justify taking him or her into care. Consultation indicates that 'with reference to 19 year old Jacques Becker it is evident that he was left very free. He could go out and come back at the hours he wished, thus he did not feel either loved or directed.' Ali Benamon 'enjoyed a large measure of freedom where his family was concerned, he was subject to no parental authority. Severe sanctions were necessary – perhaps an authoritarian placement through the organisation *Accueil et promotion des étrangers.*' Mme Bouchet, for her part, who 'is devoted to her son and excused nearly all his faults, is the reason why Jacques, 14 years old, is fixated on her in a very infantile way, and is incapable of reflecting on the consequences of his actions'. The centre recommends sending him to a direct Pedagogical Institute of Educational Supervision (IPES).

Michel B., 'very attached to his mother who is extremely overprotective', will be placed in a home. Claude D., 'very spoiled by a mother who has lost two children was, as a result of his mother's overprotection and the absence of his father, who was in a sanatorium, left free to his own devices'. It was recommended that he be sent to an IPES in the centre of France.

Again and again we find this unbeatable double classification of overprotection/rejection from which no family can escape and the sequence of rationalisation which allows the disqualification of the minor and his family is always the same:

Overprotective environment	absence of identification
father and mother permissive	absence of Oedipal resolution
father and mother authoritarian	absence of identification
flight, delinquency = expression of an emotional claim	separation from the environment, placement in a 'closed and comprehensive centre'.

professional apprenticeship   army
                              repeated running   prison
                              away
                              recidivism
                              re-assimilation
                              into the ordered
                              system

One arrives at the notion of overprotection – generally maternal overprotection – by stressing the real or symbolic absence of the father (in hospital, in prison or frequently away, overwhelmed or exhausted by work, etc.). This entails a preponderant role for the mother, or even identification with her. It can also be arrived at through interpretation of the attitude of non-collaboration of one or both of the parents with the social or legal services: 'She excuses her son's faults.'

One arrives at the theory of rejection on the same basis: the absence of a father leads to a desperate quest for an identificatory focus, in the absence of the natural one. Or one can identify rejection purely and simply with a permissive education in which too much liberty is left to the child.

A request for placement made by the family of course provides ideal grounds for an interpretation in terms of rejection.

These processes are clearly unconscious: François Clément is 15 years old 'his truanting and his stealing are significant: the delinquency here reveals an emotional disturbance, rejection of the environment, even if the rest of the family is not conscious of this feeling. It is all very understandable: François has no mother ... What is more François only got the chance to integrate himself emotionally with this family at the age of 9, that is to say at an age when the ego is blocked. His impulsive reactions such as his truancies express the agressiveness of a child lacking education. He must therefore be considered as a small boy who needs attentive supervision and some reassuring contact with an adult. The possibility of hormone treatment will be reviewed in a few months.' François then spends three years in a centre for trade apprenticeship.

Whether rejected or overprotected, the child is 'left to his own devices'. Such is the case of Serge Thiebard: 'his parents are overwhelmed with work, Serge has enormous difficulties in the relational sphere, which leads to repercussions in his behaviour, which can be lucid or sullen. Too dependent on the maternal image, Serge cannot identify with a father who remains distant and foreign to his own preoccupations. The non-resolution of the Oedipus complex and the difficulties of paternal identification will lead to ambivalence in the sexual sphere.'

Medico-psychological investigation thus produces an all-encompassing and incontrovertible criterion for legal intervention. It is incontrovertible on several counts: any defensiveness shared in common by parents and children faced with the legal apparatus is considered to be pathologically hyperprotective; any distance between parents and children, in fact or imposed by the conditions of life and work, is a rejection, generating frustrations and the destruction of the personality. Each concrete factor in the mutual attitudes of parents and children is liable to a reversible, all-encompassing and double-edged interpretation. And when concrete evidence is lacking, recourse to the symbolic makes good the lack. Finally – and this is not unimportant – the psychological investigation denies the minor and his family any possibility of replying, of inserting their own views on themselves into the process of legal investigation: although it may be possible to prove that one feeds one's children well and that one sends them to school, or that they have not stolen this motorbike from that spot, there is no way of demonstrating that one does provide an identificatory focus, nor that one has correctly 'resolved one's Oedipus complex'.

MEASURES

On the basis of the social enquiry or medico-psychological investigations, the children's magistrate or the juvenile court may take three types of measure: warning, supervision of the environment, or confinement.

The warning can be a 'reprimand' (in criminal law) or a 'return to the family' (in criminal or civil law). Both are pronounced by the children's magistrate alone, in 'closed court' and consist essentially in a homily designed to obtain from the minor and his family the expression of a firm resolution not to do it again. It is in effect in their interest to comply, because, although these warning measures may appear benign and old-fashioned, they nevertheless figure in the minor's criminal records (if they have an origin in criminal law) or in the files of the juvenile court. That is to say, and there is here a point in common between children's justice and ordinary justice, that recidivism automatically entails the application of a more serious measure, of supervision of the environment or confinement.

In good and bad years alike, such cautionary measures account for half of the decisions given in Lille and Valenciennes.[14]

The ways of supervising the environment are probation (a criminal measure), AEMO and guardianship of special welfare payments (measures of protection). The magistrate fixes the duration. Where it is a matter of protection, it is legally cancelled if the minor marries, is freed, attains the age of majority or enters the army.

The probation measure consists essentially in supervising the work and leisure activities of the minor, in ensuring the collaboration of his family in successfully carrying out this probation and in involving the headmaster of the child's school or his employer. If the minor persists in his manifestations of independence, if he refuses to submit to these controls or if his family obstructs the measure, the probation officer informs the children's magistrate and requests him to initiate the 'probation problem' procedure. By virtue of his right to go back on his earlier decision at any moment, the magistrate – or the court – then pronounces a heavier penalty.[15]

Probation may furthermore be accompanied by a further measure, to make it more of a constraint: placement in a boarding school or in a home, or a suspended prison sentence.

In such cases it is a matter of exercising a control more particularly centred on the minor himself, and designed to bring heavy pressure to bear on him, in order to keep him on a straight and narrow path. The court is, as it were, made present in the housing estate, constituting a kind of permanent threat. However, it must be recognised that this threat is often a quite derisory one, that the probation officers are few enough in number, and that except for the cases in which they persist with determination they add little enough to the supervision and threat already exercised by the police in working-class areas.

The situation is rather different where measures of AEMO are concerned. These represent one-third of the children's magistrate's decisions for 'protection' and for guardianship of social welfare payments, which accompany these in one case in three.

It is not surprising to find that AEMO and guardianship are prescribed first and foremost for families where social enquiries have drawn attention to numerous transgressive elements of behaviour such as fluid sociability, providing a refuge for delinquency, irregular work, etc.

As they are applied to the least integrated families and aim to transform their daily behaviour, it is not surprising that the duration of these measures is particularly long. They are generally prescribed for a period of three years and are indefinitely renewable, at least so long as there is an under-age child in the house to 'protect'. Given that such action takes place within the general environment, it is likewise natural that these measures should be the cornerstone for the collection and use of information concerning these families, and for the coordination of the efforts of the educational, medical, social, and housing authorities and of the police.

This exchange of information, increase of supervision, and interrelationship between the activities of all those who directly establish guidelines for the environment and manage its occupants, produces a tightly meshed net in which irregular families cannot fail to find themselves more or less totally ensured. The medical social worker of the regional hospital centre informs the children's magistrate that the X. children are in danger, the parents refuse to place Eric, 6 years old, in a sanatorium. Following a social enquiry the magistrate makes an AEMO order. Soon after M. X. falls into debt notably with rent arrears, as he has been several months without work. The Slum Clearance Programme (PACT) threatens eviction, notifies the medical social worker charged with the AEMO order and requests an order for guardianship which it obtains.

At home, under the thumb of the AEMO, the guardian and PACT, the X.s are the object of solicitude on the part of the educational social worker, and her district colleague, both of whom have been alerted by their colleagues in court. However, it should not be imagined that a constant stream of inquisitors beats a path to their door. Supervision is not always present, far from it. It is simply that the X.s are 'known to the services', who have their eye on them, and their mistakes are quickly noted.

Apart from setting up this kind of 'social record', parallel to the police record, but fuller, the first effect of the AEMO measure is to kill all manifestations of exuberance or waywardness in these families and to create a vacuum around them. In some cases this is indeed its only effect: it puts a stop to the accommodation of strangers in the family, to outings for the parents and to freedom allowed to the children. Money is meted out in dribs and drabs so as to cut short any tendencies towards independence and to enforce a programme of regular work. All this cannot be achieved in a day. To be successful, one must from time to time brandish the threat of placement for the children, remind the family that one represents the court, occasionally even summon it there⁻ for a statutory lecture.

Next, one must make the situation secure, prevent the family from profiting from any relaxation of control to reconstitute its former way of life. The family must be made to get used to being supervised: weekly or fortnightly, according to whim, the social worker comes without warning, often with the sole aim of remaining informed, of reminding them of her existence and that she knows many things learnt through such and such a social service, or the police or the department of public prosecutions. When the situation is desperate, no more than a purely supervisory activity of this kind is attempted. The Jonquères live in extreme wretchedness. Monsieur is drowning in alcohol at a rate of knots. Their living quarters are falling to pieces. So the supervisors just wait for cirrhosis to carry off the husband, or for him to be sacked from work or for him to half-kill his wife as he sometimes sets out to do, whereupon they will be empowered to take further steps. For the moment they prevent the children who are already placed from returning to their parents' home, they try to convince the mother herself to place one or two others in order to protect them from her husband, and they make sure that she does not go off with another man....

With younger families, or those less obviously crushed by poverty, AEMO has more dynamic plans: not simply to supervise but to convert. In such cases the combination of AEMO and financial guardianship produces its full effect, especially since for many families the sum of the social benefits they may receive equals or is greater than that of their wages.

It is a matter of combining management of the family's behaviour with educational assistance and management of their means of existence through financial guardianship. The guardian (who prefers to be known as a delegate from the social benefit) first sets out to manage the family food expenses: it is she who goes to pay the grocer, the baker and the butcher. Over and above the supervision thus exercised over possible family splurges it is a question of getting them used to keeping accounts of their spending, and submitting these for approval to the social worker.

On this basis, and acting in concert with the social worker, the guardian proposes rehousing, which can take several forms: if the husband is sick, or in irregular work, or particularly poorly paid, or too old, they offer the family social accommodation, generally PACT, which has at its disposal groups of apartments in old houses that have been converted. They thus place the family in reserves for people in care which constitute a new type of courtyard complex, visited daily by this or that social service, and at the same time they cut it off from its home territory. This opportunity also makes it possible to place the family under the control of a lodging-house organisation which has its own social service and which is particularly vigilant in the matter of regular payment of rents. This may, in exceptional cases, lead to promotion to HLM housing (Habitations à loyer modéré: low-rent housing).

If the husband is earning a 'good' living, if he is young and in good health, the social worker and the financial guardian guide the family in the direction of building or buying a house that they will eventually own. The family is thus moved into an aseptic environment where it is fixed, because of the payment of rent instalments, for the rest of its life.

Once the family has been thus displaced, the AEMO calls on the financial guardianship to organise a good use of the housing: the guardian or supervisor makes economies to buy new furniture and a television, so that she can rest assured that the family is at last settled somewhere. Then they get the parents used to using the appropriate leisure institutions: family holiday villages for family vacations, holiday camps for the children. The family is then well on the way to socialisation.

What remains is to retain control for a few more years, to ensure that the family has at last become integrated in a new pattern of behaviour and, given that the family's development is never linear and that in the passing of time there is always some sort of relapse (a child who steals or runs away) there is always a reason for prolonging the legal intervention, or for punctuating it with temporary placements, in order finally to achieve definitive adherence or submission to the system.

MUTED BARBARITY

The system of evaluation and intervention organised around the children's court is obsessed with the family. Its rules and reflexes are to make it healthy, to redress it, to educate it, to convert or reconstitute it because 'one must never lose faith in the inspiration of the family'.[16] It is almost always with regret that a magistrate or a social service exterminates a family, by dispersing all the children to various placement centres, by pushing the parents towards psychiatric hospitalisation or prison or by supporting a court decision for forfeiture of parental authority. If one does not grasp the extent to which this obsession with the family directs the perceptions and practices of the socio-legal services, one runs great risk of not perceiving the reasons behind certain major contradictions between their practice and their intentions.

I have suggested on the subject of juvenile delinquency that the absence of gravity in most of the cases, makes it no more than a pretext for a 'pedagogical' intervention which most frequently extends to the delinquent's family. Affairs which might have been settled with the pronouncement of a fine or an obligation to make civil compensation for damages caused instead become, through the intercession of a social enquiry and medico-psychological examinations, the point of departure for interminable measures of re-education for the families concerned. Conversely, in serious matters, notably cases of murder, the medico-psychological evidence is discounted, and leaves the entire arena to the penal code's understanding of the facts. In the case of ordinary delinquency, psychiatric expertise or vocational guidance consultation always leads to a diagnosis and a diminution of the offence in the analysis of the delinquent's environment and family history. In direct inverse proportion in the courts of assizes, psychiatry almost always beats a retreat before the laws of justice. The experts conclude that the delinquent is responsible and liable to the penal sanctions against all probability, particularly in view of the criteria which they themselves habitually retain in order to pronounce a minor 'irresponsible'. After all, what explanation can there be for them declaring responsible for his acts and liable to penal sanctions a murderer of $15\frac{1}{2}$ years old, who is disabled, illiterate, the eldest of a large family in which it is impossible to tell whether there are too many or too few

fathers, and whose dossier indicates that he has been denied
schooling from a very young age because of his disability,
disturbance and violence?

In spite of its declared intentions, the system of medico-
psychological interpretation does not in any way alleviate the
situation of these minors faced with the judicial apparatus. On
the contrary, it helps to extend the power of that apparatus
over the children and their families, by transforming the follies
of youth into symptoms of pathological disorder. And at the
same time it also increases the gravity of the charge pressing on
a criminal minor, by withdrawing its sanction from any
endeavour to relate the actions of such a delinquent to his
history, even while still claiming to retain a monopoly over
such attempts. This retraction would be inexplicable or at least
paradoxical, without the family obsession which I have mentioned above. In the same way that the juvenile court is in
reality a family court, the psychiatry – or psychology – of the
child is that of its framework. And it is this framework that is
the unit for observation and intervention. If the crime of one of
the children can help to re-stabilise the family because it is
relieved of one of the most troubled of its members, if the crime
can be used to terrorise the family to force it to return to the
straight and narrow or (if this is too hard for it) lead it into
autodestruction, what is the point of taking account of and
understanding the unique circumstances of a 15-year-old
murderer? The same process occurs in cases of 'battered
babies', a theme recurrent in the mass media which generally
discovers that the 'scandal' has taken place in a family known
to the social services and condemns their inadequate reactions.
How can it be that the social services, whose task is to watch
over 'the physical and moral health, and the education and
safety of children', have allowed children they have seen several
times a month to be battered, sometimes even killed? How can
a little girl of 4 years be killed by being trampled underfoot in a
family which is actively known to three magistrates, a doctor,
two medical social workers and an investigator, and despite the
warnings given by a teacher and a headmistress, and six legal

interventions?[17] Should one, in accordance with the line taken by the press, believe that social workers are either incompetent or overworked?

Actually, it is inconceivable that the official visitors to irregular families should not know when a child is being badly battered. But, here again, the eye takes in not what it sees, but rather what it is looking for: the situation is evaluated in the perspective of the education of the family as a whole, and in the light of an analysis of its economy. If the bad treatment meted out to a child – often from an earlier marriage – makes it possible for the couple and other children to find an equilibrium and an outlet, it must be considered as a functional element in the process of family intervention, and although not approved of, it is tolerated, because it is useful. If the withdrawal or restitution of the child can, for one or both of the parents, have the effect of providing pressure conducive to the stabilisation of the couple or, in a more general manner, to imposing upon it the court and social services' own view of their responsibilities, then the possible withdrawal or restitution of the child is exploited even if this exacerbates the ambivalent feelings of the parents with respect to a child which brings them so many complications and vexations. It then sometimes happens that, in this war against irregular families, the hostage dies, because the resistance of children is not inexhaustible and the social services' obsession with the family has prevented them from seeing that the critical threshold had been reached. The hostage dies not despite the protection of the law, but because of that protection, because of the solicitude of these experts on misfortune, education and the law, because their obsession renders them professionally myopic, incapable of finding water in the sea or a tree in a forest. In the ultimate analysis, then, protection entails a sort of muted barbarity, exercised by people above suspicion, whose responsibilities are diluted by a bureaucracy which then proceeds to make the affair redound to its own credit as it proclaims that those who cannot see owe their blindness purely and simply to their lack of means and the inadequacy of their apparatus.

5

INDIVIDUAL CASES UNDER
SCRUTINY

Everyone knows the admirable pages in which Fenimore Cooper, the Walter Scott of America, depicts the ferocious customs of the savages, their picturesque, poetic language, the thousand ruses by which they kill or trap their enemies. We are going to try to put before the eyes of the reader a few episodes from the lives of other barbarians, as far removed from civilisation as the savage peoples so well painted by Cooper. However, the barbarians of which we speak are in our midst, we can rub shoulders with them by venturing into the dens they inhabit. These men have their own habits, their own women, a mysterious language full of significant expressions.

(Eugène Sue, *Les Mystères de Paris*)

The following tale of a voyage among the barbarians 'in our midst' was written in the course of visits made in the company of social workers, educators or the financial guardians of social benefits carrying out AEMO recommendations made by a children's magistrate. The author, presenting himself as an outside observer visiting the court, as indeed he was, was considered by the families as yet another official sent by the judge – just one of many. He was able to avail himself of the position usually reserved for a student, to attempt to make himself the Fenimore Cooper for irregular families and the missionaries bent on civilising them.

The time is 5.30 p.m.; it has rained all day, it is icy cold, and the complex – three rows of low housing belonging to PACT – is even more dismal than you would expect. The social benefits' financial supervisor is expected at the end house on the right, the home of the Watrins, four children from 13 years to thirteen months, the father an invalid in the scrap business and a skinny wife dedicated to housework. Not long ago they

all lived together in one room. PACT has requested, and
obtained, a supervisory financial order because they have not
been paying the 150 francs monthly rent. The district social
worker has obtained an AEMO, judging the children to be in
danger. The Watrins are thus regularly visited by a social
worker from the court, who is the daughter and the wife of
influential local industrialists, and by the social benefits'
supervisor, who has for the past two years been rather wonder-
ing what on earth she is doing there.

The three oldest children are on holiday, in Salvation Army
camps. They normally go conscientiously to school, and no one
could tell me why the district social worker considered them to
be in moral danger. The Watrin house has three rooms, one
above the other. The bottom one gives directly onto the central
bay of the court. In the course of his scrap dealing, M. Watrin
has been able to furnish it with an enormous ornate and
overloaded sideboard, two old television sets – one or the other
of which may be in working order – a table, a few chairs and a
coal stove on which a clothes boiler is bubbling. A cat is tied to
a chair, 'because she mustn't go out and get pregnant', says
Mme Watrin. Her husband has vanished; he does not like
social workers. Mme Watrin gives her report: the children are
well. They have written postcards which she takes out of an old
biscuit tin and gives to the financial supervisor to read 'Love
and kises. I am well. The weather is good.' The younger –
thirteen months old – babbles happily in her mother's arms.
'Have you found any more cockroaches?' 'No, I bought a spray
and I have sprayed everywhere.' She shows the spray in case
they don't believe her.

'Is your husband going to buy a washing machine soon?'

'Well, he says that, at the moment, the scrap business is
failing.'

'Yes but, after all, he is not the one who does the washing, is
he? What would he say if he had to do his scrap dealing on a
bicycle instead of in his van?'

Silence. The walls are covered with photographs of the
children, two girls, two boys.

The room is always dark, perhaps a dozen square metres. Mme Watrin dives again into her biscuit tin and takes out an official document stating that her husband will henceforth be considered as an invalid of the first category, in other words, able to exercise a remunerative activity: 'We have the honour to inform you etc. ...' In consequence, his annual pension is docked by one third. About 3,000 francs remains. No one gets upset.

'You should go to the social security office. Here, I'll give you a form.'

M. Watrin makes about 600 francs a month with his scrap dealing. He has a stomach ulcer. He can't drink. He can manage. He would like them to leave him in peace. Once the social worker came when he was there; he thought she was boney and prim. He asked her if she had any children. 'Why, Monsieur, what has that to do with you?' Since then he never fails to make up to her or subject her to a string of obscenities. He doesn't give a damn for her, he has nothing against her but prefers not to have to see her. The conversation begins to languish. No one is sitting down. A few pleasantries to the baby, to fill the silence, and then; 'Didn't you go out this weekend? Don't you make the most of not having the children at home to go on a lovers' stroll?'

Mme Watrin smiles wanly: 'No, you see, yesterday, we ate at 7.30 and by 8.30 we were fast asleep.'

'Right, well, that's it. Give my regards to your husband.' More joking with the baby whose mother is feeding her again. No one shakes hands, we all pretend to smile. Nothing has happened; the visit lasted twenty minutes.

Roubaix: a dwelling provided by PACT, opposite the monstrous factories of Armand Motte's spinning mills, now taken over by Phildar; a brick entrance porch at least twelve metres high, and behind, gigantic brick workshops, neither red nor brown, just dirty. The apartment comes as a surprise; it is quite large and bright. It is reached by a staircase which make one's legs ache, and a very narrow corridor. Two rooms on the upper floor and two others beneath, at the bottom of another precipitous staircase. The children are away; two are with their great aunt and two in an IMP (Medico-Pedagogical Institute). There is no one here but Mme Verbruges, her lover and a remarkably affectionate dog. We are received without embarrassment, in a friendly if not cordial fashion. The social worker and the financial supervisor have given warning of their visit. Their problem is to find a solution for the two children placed in the IMP who have not come out since last Christmas, that is to say six months ago. The educational team of the IMP would like them to spend two days with their mother and also to see their father. But Mme Verbruges does not want to see 'Monsieur Verbruges' (as she calls him) any more than M. Verbruges wants to see her.

Last December, Mme Verbruges killed her youngest child, David, aged nine months, by thumping him against a door, during a fit of hysterics. The couple had been rehoused in a 'housing estate' inhabited by numerous alcoholics, M. Verbruges, who had just emerged from a drying-out cure, had relapsed into drinking with them. A neighbour, with the reputation of a troublemaker, had made advances to him. Mme Verbruges, constantly under pressure and receiving a psychiatric disability pension, killed her son one day when he had been howling all day for no apparent reason.

She had spent four months in prison and was waiting to come up for trial at 'the Douai Assizes, which was a serious matter. The examining magistrate had not deemed primitive action appropriate. But he had allowed four months to pass before setting Mme Verbruges at provisional liberty. From Christmas to Easter, Mme Verbruges had thus been in prison, at Loos, writing unceasingly to her children. Psychiatrists came from Paris, and found that her responsibility was 'partially diminished'. Counsel was provided for her through legal aid.

The children's magistrate was waiting for the Court of Assizes before pronouncing on the children's fate. Meanwhile, a provisional care order entrusted two of them to M. Verbruges's aunt, and Mme Verbruges saw them no more; all she could do was write to them. She did not want to see the family of her husband who was a boozer and idler. In addition, the aunt had been kind enough to tell the two children in the IMP that their mother had killed their little brother.

Mme Verbruges offers chairs. She immediately comes into the attack: she wants her children, everything is ready to receive them. 'Can I see?' asks the financial supervisor. 'Certainly.' Their room is ready and decorated. Only the beds are lacking. They will buy them when they are sure that the judge will return the children. The lover, M. Sénat, agrees. He is as placid and silent as Mme Verbruges is mobile and talkative. But the children's magistrate cannot decide. He is waiting for the Assize Court. It is not even known on what date it will try Mme Verbruges. Not before October in any case. Between now and then, Thierry and Dominique must have an opportunity to come out of the IMP but this must be to see both their father and their mother, and the father is in a home for alcoholics. Can Mme Verbruges take the children for a weekend and entrust them to the father for an afternoon? Big fuss: 'I don't want to see him again. That would really cause trouble. M. Sénat will bash his face in.' M. Sénat doesn't want to bash anyone's face in, but M. Verbruges is a troublemaker. The other day he came and threatened him from the street. M. Sénat works regularly as a stripper, that is a cleaner of carding machines in a mill. The social worker asks him to describe his work and asks him what hours he works. Just a way of making sure he really is working?

Mme Verbruges is getting worked up: yes, M. Sénat is ready to welcome the children as if they were his own; yes, she is more than fed up with always being told to wait; yes, they are always soft-soaping her and doing nothing. What's more, she has just been denied her invalid's pension and been told to be re-examined. 'I won't go. I'm fed up with doctors.' She's had it anyway. Her husband has messed it all up by going back to the bottle and not working. She had saved 200 francs to buy furniture; he took it all for drink.

One of M. Sénat's brothers arrives. He wants to give

everyone his advice, because he knows the law and he was a shop steward when he worked at Roubaix: the social worker meanwhile wants to know only one thing: if the IMP sends Thierry and Dominique to their mother one Friday, will she let her husband come to see them on Sunday and take them for a walk? 'If he doesn't come up but waits for them at the door, yes. And if he doesn't bring them back at the agreed time, I will call the cops.' In passing, Mme Verbruges speaks her mind about the cops.

The two social workers tease her about her hot temper and take their leave. Mme Verbruges looks grim, M. Sénat is as reserved as ever. His brother is coming to the end of a long explanation about the necessity of writing immediately to the new Minister.

Meanwhile the IMP which is housing Thierry and Dominique puts in a request for a permanent care order, because M. Verbruges is no longer working and has neither family allowance nor pension coming in. The Assize Court is on holiday; the children's magistrate is waiting for the Assize Court. Two social workers use all their ingenuity to ease the relations between M. Verbruges who is finishing his umpteenth detoxication cure and his wife who will perhaps soon be in prison, and all this will be enough for the children's magistrate to entrust the care of Thierry and Dominique permanently to the IMP.

There is also a divorce action in the air, which should pronounce on the custody of the children. It will all take a year or two at least.

After leaving Mme Verbruges's home we visit Monsieur in the 'Free Life' home.[1] He has made his will and given it to the medical social worker. He does not want his children to go to his wife 'because she has a lover, and because, with what she has done, she doesn't deserve it'. For three-quarters of an hour, the two visitors try to make him change his decision. 'Do not think of yourself, think of your children', they keep saying.

He would like them to come to the home, where they could live, and continues to refuse to let them go to his wife's home. For the sake of peace and quiet, he agrees to defer his permanent decision: he will go to see the social worker in her office. Tuesday at 4 p.m. Panic! Mme Verbruges has just announced her visit for the same day and the same time. They ask M. Verbruges not to come until 5.30 p.m.

Rémi fell into a potato machine while he was working unofficially for a farmer in Quesnoy-sur-Deule. His mother is a prostitute in Lille, who has entrusted her children to their grandmother as each one was born. Accordingly, no one is any longer sure how long the social workers have been keeping an eye on the family, or quite why, but it seems like forever, and perfectly natural.

After his accident, Rémi had a leg amputated and the court sent an educational advisor to see him, to help him prepare his future. The advisor was in favour of sending Rémi to a specialist centre. Rémi wheedled so as not to leave his village and his mother, and he won. Then the advisor persuaded him to go and live with his sister in Lille during the week, near the offices of a Kines Therapist. Rémi did not put up with that for long, in a cramped appartment in a town where he knew no one. He returned to Quesnoy and, for several weeks, threatened the advisor with his shotgun. 'This is a withdrawn boy, who is slovenly and trusts no one. He has no plans for the future, except to live on the disability pension he is hoping for.'

It is a low, one-storied house at the end of a dirt track, almost, but not completely, lost in the fields. Rémi is not there; his sister says that he is at his therapist's at Lille. No doubt this is just in a manner of speaking. The crippled grandmother, with a huge stomach and bloodshot eyes, is leaning her elbows on the table and gazing into space. Her hearing is very poor, one has to shout to make her understand. There are two chairs and an old cabinet. The educational advisor makes some harmless remarks about the weather. The girl says yes, no, perhaps. The grandmother absently mutters something or other. The absence of conversation becomes oppressive.

'And Pascal, is he there?'

'Yes, he's there.'

Help at last: 'Perhaps you could go and look for him?' Pascal comes in through a back door. Are there many more children in other rooms, waiting until the advisor has gone before they show their faces? Pascal is about 20. Handshakes all round. 'Well then, the weather's fine, what are you up to at the moment? Are you slaving away?'

'No, I'm not working any longer, I didn't get on with the boss any more. I left.'

'So what are you doing?'

'Well, I'm repapering the kitchen.' The instructor is shown the repapering and comments favourably. 'And after that?' 'Well, I've received some army papers, I'll show you them.' The papers are lost, and the advisor lectures him: 'Take care, it may be your call-up, they'll take you for a deserter.' Pascal is not too upset at the idea of being taken for a deserter. He asks if we can help him get a wheelchair from the social services for his grandmother who can't get about any longer. He shows the forms, which the instructor puts in his briefcase saying that he'll do something about them. 'And Brigitte?' 'I don't know. I don't see her so much these days.'

'Have you been to see her father?' 'No, not yet.' 'You know you ought to?' 'Yeah.' 'What does Brigitte want? To get married?' 'Yeah.' 'And you?' 'Well, not much. In any case I'll be off to the army, we'll see about it afterwards.'

'Yes, well, of course, it's your decision, but you should go and see her father. She is pregnant, after all.'

'Yeah.' Silence. The visit goes on and on; in the end the instructor takes his leave.

In the car he explains to me that they are spineless, no powers of resistance. Rémi is letting himself go. I ask if anyone is doing anything about getting damages for the accident from the farmer, or getting the disability pension etc. No, no one is doing that. We keep an eye on it from a distance through the district social worker, whose business it is. But no one is pushing too hard, in fact they are rather holding back. 'You see all that Rémi tells himself is that once he gets his pension, he'll be able to twiddle his thumbs in the sunshine.'

The Dulac family is a special case; in which there is financial supervision over welfare benefits but no welfare benefits. The family allowance office will in fact no longer pay out benefits because M. Dulac is not working; but a hire-purchase company has obtained an order of guardianship because of unpaid instalments. In addition to guardianship under a financial supervisor the Dulacs are under the provisions of an AEMO.

The house is of medium size, in the condition to be expected of a home which houses a score of children, the youngest under 5 and the oldest scarcely more than 20. The twenty children are those of two women, two sisters. When he married the one, M. Dulac found the other came with the dowry and the two sisters have often found themselves pregnant simultaneously: the legal spouse thirteen times, the other seven. The house has four or five rooms and a muddy courtyard of 200 square metres in which half a dozen dogs are noisily fighting. The children appear from all over the place – lively, laughing, relaxed accomplices. They shake hands with the two social workers in a kind of mocking dance, profiting from the confusion created by their numbers, to get themselves greeted several times over. Then they disperse, return in clusters, continuing to play among themselves, and from time to time casting a derisory glance at the group of talking adults.

Mme Dulac does not sit down, but stays in front of her stove, from time to time checking the stewpan where the lunch is simmering. She smiles all the time, passing her hand over a child's head, looking at the courtyard, smilingly telling the latest escapade of her smallest toddler. Her thirteen pregnancies have thickened her, but she retains an enormous vitality, and is at the same time calm yet jolly. The two social workers have come to give her an account of their administrative efforts with the family allowance office to get the family allowance payments paid again. Now that two of the older children are working, it seems that they may be successful. The allocations were withdrawn because M. Dulac, who stopped working four years ago and has been producing medical certificates – suspected of being forgeries – has not been recognised as either ill or invalid by the competent authority. M. Dulac is furious, he loathes social workers and shuts himself in a room when they come. 'You wouldn't do a thing like that, Madame Dulac', says the social worker. 'I'm not so rude that I close my door when someone rings', she replies, remaining pleasant but making it clear that this is a matter of etiquette and nothing more. She suggests sending someone to find M. Dulac, who has been listening behind the door and bursts in at full speed, before anyone can make a move. He is very excited, his voice is so hoarse that one can hardly hear him. Without preamble, and even while shaking hands, he turns on the two social workers. 'I know for sure that you're against me, that you're telling everyone I can work and I'm telling you fibs. But deep down you know perfectly well that I'm sick. I'm 49 years old, thirty-five years in the building trade. My legs have given up, I can't even do 500 metres on foot.' The social welfare guardian makes fun of him, tells him not to indulge so much in listening to the sound of his own voice.

In fact, M. Dulac has a perfecly clear view of the situation. He has toiled for thirty-five years, he wants to stop; he has enough children of working age for that. Let them take over, he's had enough. Only, now that the children earn the family money, M. Dulac is increasingly losing his importance. They don't ask his advice, his wife takes decisions with the two who work, he is pushed aside in his own family, relegated to his room with his bottle of rum, or sits in front of the television. No one blames him, no one is reproaching him, it's just that he hardly seems to count any more. So, he takes his revenge as he can, he reminds them that he's there by shouting at them all. His children want to put up wall-paper on the kitchen walls on Sunday and have fun on Saturday. He forbids it: 'It's Saturday you work and Sunday you play.' One of his sons, physically handicapped, gets about in a little car for which a brother has bought an engine. He forbids anyone to use it: it is too dangerous: the invalid will go and get involved with mopeds and there will be an accident. None of these prohibitions carry much weight, it's perfectly obvious that in the long run the children will repaper the kitchen on the day of their choice and that the invalid will have his car, but it is a war of attrition. After all this, M. Dulac will find something else. There's nothing tragic about the situation. Mme Dulac never loses her good humour, nor the children their joyful high spirits.

The financial supervisor tries to persuade M. Dulac to work, to give up his claims of being an invalid, given that the commission won't recognise him as such. M. Dulac produces a medical certificate and talks of serious liver and nervous complaints. The social worker puts it in his bag. It will be sent to the right person. But all this will in no way alter the fact that, at the request of some hire-purchase firm, the jolly Mme Dulac, her husband who doesn't want to work any more, and twenty children bursting with health, curiosity and vitality, have for at least three years been subject to an AEMO and a social benefit guardianship order.

The atmosphere relaxes. Even so, M. Dulac returns to the question of repapering the kitchen. 'Isn't it true that you shouldn't work on Sunday? Besides, you wouldn't work on Sunday would you?' he says to the social worker. 'But I do, M. Dulac, at the moment I'm in the middle of digging my garden to make a terrace. I was at it all day Sunday and my hands are covered with blisters.' He shows them, and Mme Dulac literally chokes with laughter. 'I only said it for something to say', says M. Dulac, who is also in fits of laughter at this office worker trying to fraternise through his blisters. Another look around before leaving; the children reappear from every corner and take up their position on the doorstep to watch the 2CV Citroen drive away.

The Jonquères live in Armentières in a house they have been trying to buy which still contains a few pieces of furniture; the whole place is slowly falling to bits. Mme Jonquère has ten children. She is 35 years old, but seems older. To say she looks old is putting it mildly: she is in a state of fatigue, poverty and resignation which has stamped her with a crushed appearance, ageless and sexless. The social worker couldn't say how long

the social services have been interested in the Jonquère family.
What with the family allowance office, custody, the district, the
court, the mother and child service and mental welfare, the
Jonquères were probably born with a social worker and will
die with one too.

The room which serves as the dining-room is long and
narrow, about eight metres by two. Mme Jonquère puts out a
chair for the social worker at one end and one for herself at the
other. Two boys and two girls move silently around the chairs.
The boys, 3 and 6 years old, are naked and black with mud and
dust. Their mother doesn't dress them, so they don't go to play
in the street. What is left for them is the house and a small
enclosed courtyard of perhaps 100 square metres. Mme Jonquère has been back from hospital for eight days. Her husband
was the cause of her being there, after a particularly brutal
beating. He works from time to time and drinks a lot, chalking
up large debts in cafés. One son has been abandoned, two girls
are placed, another son is in a medical training college. Mme
Jonquère was a former ward of national assistance, made to
work like a beast of burden by a foster family from the age of 14.

From her end of the room, the social worker tries to make
Mme Jonquère talk. 'When he beat you, were the children
here?' 'Yes, the three here and their brother Bruno.'

'How did they react?'

'They were scared. And now, they hide as soon as their
father begins to shout.'

'And is he often drunk, these days?'

'Not too much, he's working again, he was scared after
beating me up. He had never beaten me like that before. I
refused to make it up with him.'

'And Maryse, is she going to come back?'

'I don't know. She wrote that she'd really like to. She is due
for leave from Saint-Omer.'

'Do you think it wise for her to come back?' Silence.

'And Dominique, don't you think that he'll be better off in
the IMP with his brother?' (Dominique is 6 years old and is
backward at talking.)

'Oh dear, I don't know, he's naughty.'

The social worker's plan is simple; the situation of the Jonquères is a dead end: the father is too soaked in drink, too irregularly employed. The social welfare financial supervisor can change the food and clothing. But of all the children the happiest one is surely the boy who has been abandoned and adopted. As for those who are placed, they should be left where they are and family contact severed. If one or two others can be placed, so much the better. As for Maryse, a visit will be made to Saint-Omer to see her instructors in order to persuade her to stay there, press on as quickly as possible with her training, and burn her bridges. But Maryse wants to go back home. If her mother can be persuaded to tell her not to come back, perhaps she will change her mind. But the mother has nothing to say on that score. She agrees when the social worker talks of the dangers for a 16-year-old girl close to an alcoholic father, who has already tried to interfere with her in a corner. She acquiesces when the social worker evokes the trauma which a girl undergoes in seeing her father manhandling her mother. But when she is on the point of saying what she is going to do, whether she is going to see Maryse to persuade her to stay at Saint-Omer, she becomes evasive. She talks about something else, complains about the length of the journey, the cost, her fatigue. She will think about it. As she shows her out, she still manages a few friendly words for the social worker ...

The Dupuis parents were accused of battering their children. The educational social worker brought them to the court's attention. An enquiry was made from which it transpired that the battering was an invention of neighbours, exasperated by Mme Dupuis's noisy irritability in the two rooms in which she was bringing up six children. The court nevertheless ordered an AEMO precisely because of this irritability. After which the Dupuis family were accommodated by HLM (Habitation à loyer modéré – a body which provides subsidised housing for people in need).

M. Dupuis is in the middle of repairing his 2CV. Madame is

out shopping. Three boys are playing trains, in a spotless
kitchen. Mme Dupuis seems to be very houseproud. 'Too
much so', says the social worker, as if families of this kind, so
frequenty neglectful, are only clean through some neurosis just
as disturbing as disorder would bè. M. Dupuis has had bad
problems at work, which are now over. Mme Dupuis has had
many children, very close together. She found them difficult to
cope with. Even though now better housed she remains very
bad-tempered. The social worker comes to calm her, to get her
to be more level-headed, to help her to put up with her
children, above all the two boarding-school daughters who are
very excitable and noisy when they come home at weekends.

The social worker gets M. Dupuis to talk. How is his wife at
the moment? All right, out in any case, two children are
already in camps and three others leave before the end of the
month.

'Have you bought the things they need?'

'Yes, yes, it's O.K.' M. Dupuis spends his leisure time seeing
to his car and doing jobs around the house. The children play
quietly. The social worker is disappointed not to have seen
Mme Dupuis. She will call again next week.

Mme Leroux leaves the social worker at the door just long
enough for a young man to sneak out through the back. The
social worker has not seen him. Mme Leroux is in hair curlers
and dirty jeans; she is doing the housework. Despite her seven
children, she is slim, lively and supple, she has very black eyes,
fine features and a face which opens up completely as soon as
she smiles, enough confidence to feel quite at home anywhere,
and a straightforward way of talking.

Mme Leroux is a prostitute, or rather she used to be a
prostitute because for some time she hasn't asked for payment.
So the psychologists call her a nymphomaniac, but the social
worker doesn't think that is much help to her. The children are
playing in the garden, hale and hearty. Only one little girl, half
hidden behind a piece of furniture, remains to hear the
conversation. One of her sisters comes in and goes and stands in

front of the social worker. She looks her up and down and asks: 'Who is this?' 'It's the social worker,' replies the younger girl.

The social worker is here to take stock of Mme Leroux, her associates and her outings, it being agreed that it would be better for her not to go out at all. 'When I go out, I forget the time; if I meet someone I know, I talk to him, sometimes we go together, and then I come back late, and if it is after my husband, we have a row because the meal isn't ready.' Mme Leroux talks of her outings with an amused detachment. That's how it is. She is pretty and young and her seven children don't make her feel that she should live like a nun. She is not snide with the social worker; she has even asked for the AEMO measure, which is coming to an end, to be renewed. The social worker reminds her of this several times and advises her not to go out, to turn away people who seek her out at home. 'If you go on being absent for hours on end, one of your children will fall out of a window and they will take them all away from you. Especially since the neighbours ...' Mme Leroux nods her agreement. But how can she not go out, when her husband is bitter, because his brother is a big shot in Armentières and he himself is only a mere workman? A husband who wants his meal the minute he arrives home, who goes off fishing on Friday night and doesn't come back until Sunday dinner? Mme Leroux has a good plan to go to Cahors, where her brother-in-law, whom she likes a lot, has a hotel-restaurant. Down there, she could re-make her life, and would not be dogged everywhere with the reputation of a prostitute. The social worker acquiesces, as one would agree with a child saying that he will be a fireman or an astronaut when he grows up. For the moment, Mme Leroux should not go out or receive company. Exit social worker. The young man can come back in.

Why are the Willots the object of an AEMO order? Because the routine social services have picked them out, because they have debts, because they have been put under financial supervision, because Mme Willot and her daughter have been found to be too excitable. Now they are moving house: they are leaving for the Isère, where their son is already established and has found them a house and some work. Goodbye Lille, goodbye AEMO. A glass of white wine with the supervisor to celebrate the separation. 'We will send you our address; if you're passing, you must come and see us.' The house is repainted, inside and out, in order to be sold at the best price. The supervisor is there like an ornament on the mantelpiece. His only role is to listen to the cascade of words from Mme Willot and her daughter Viviane, who talk of the North, of the Isère, of beer. Viviane has had a miscarriage after a bad fall. 'You should have seen a doctor straightaway, then you might not have lost your baby.' Useless advice, useless talk. With the Willots there's a mixture of genuine friendliness and feigned cordiality where official visitors are concerned. The first glass is followed by a second. The supervisor is in a hurry to leave. M. Willot delays him again to have a paper received from the building society explained. Round and round the mulberry bush ... .

6

INDIVIDUAL CASES CORRECTED

Report on the mental examination of Claude X., by Doctor H.

I, the undersigned, Doctor H., chief physician at the psychiatric hospital of A., medical expert attached to the courts, was appointed by order of Monsieur B., Children's Magistrate for the Court of Lille, on 10 July 19..

1. To proceed with the mental examination of the minor Claude X.

2. To say:

Whether, at the time of the offences, the minor was of unsound mind, in the sense of Article 64 of the Criminal Code.

Whether he shows mental or psychiatric problems which are capable of influencing his behaviour.

Whether he is a danger to public order or to himself.

Whether the problems or deficiencies discovered require a particular measure of protection, safety, re-education, or a treatment of special care, or whether they are offset by any professional or other features.

I certify and swear that I have personally carried out these operations.

THE FACTS AND INFORMATION

The dossier: Claude, born 4 December 1954, has already been convicted for stealing in 1968. The probation officer's report mentions that the family environment is normal but that the parents are puzzled by the child's conduct. He has stolen money from a butcher, and cigarettes. Sometimes he sleeps in his parents' car. The proposal is for placement at Oxelaere, followed by a Vocational and Selection Centre (COT) at

Lambersart. The family doctor advises separation from the environment. Medico-psychological examinations have established that he is mentally retarded with personality problems. He has a verbal IQ of 60 and a performance IQ of 71.

On 16 June, he was caught hunting birds with a rifle. He had also stolen some money. He comes from a family of seven children. *The father*: he states that the child was like the others in infancy, except for being very backward at school, but that at the age of 12, he started to do silly things. He gets himself expelled from apprenticeship centres, he loafs around. It has not been possible to place him. The father thinks there may have been a grandmother who had to go to a psychiatric hospital.

EXAMINATION

Claude is a boy of medium size, slow, rough, wide-eyed, with sticking-out ears, blushing easily, untidy and dirty, with big hands.

On the surface he is emotional, but underneath remains indifferent and unmoved. He can spell out his name and give his date of birth. He says he is equally fond of his mother and father. At first sight he shows neither jealousy nor frustration vis-à-vis his brothers and sisters. He admits that he didn't like school much. His level of intelligence is indeed very low, at the mentally deficient level, with an IQ of less than 65. His moral sense is weak. He has no tastes, no particular focus of interest; he is very clumsy.

Nevertheless attempts have been made to put him in a spinning-mill apprenticeship centre, but he stole money from the manager and was expelled. He also admits that he bought a rifle, with which he killed sparrows. He found some loose change in a car. He admits that none of this is right but you have to keep at it to get through to him. He spends his time playing about with his neighbours, playing cards. Sometimes he does not come home but sleeps in the car. There have also been occasions when he has threatened his mother and told her that if she does not give him money he will steal it.

The physical examination is negative; the pulse is normal, there are no recent traces of epilepsy.

DISCUSSION

So this is a case of a mentally deficient boy, with personality problems connected in particular with educational difficulties; it is clear that the parents have lost all authority and that all attempts to provide him with work, or vocational training, have failed.

A defective of this level can normally live at home, provided there is a minimum of supervision and support, but in this case there are the habits of vagrancy, slovenliness and aggressive behaviour towards his relations. There has been talk of putting him in an observation centre and also of an apprenticeship centre. It is quite clear that an observation centre would not discover any more than has already been seen in various examinations, in other words, a rather low IQ, and educational and personality problems.

On the other hand, any normal apprenticeship centre cannot take him and such attempts have been failures. Thus two possibilities remain for him: one is a medical–vocational institute, in other words one of the often part-boarding establishments which takes backward people and occupies them in work. But it should be noted that this requires at the least a measure of discipline and the cooperation of parents. Failing that, the only solution will be that of a psychiatric hospital. However, there is still a possibility that, after a certain period of discipline and re-adaption to small tasks, he might be better prepared to go to an IMP; in any eventuality he should be under financial supervision.

CONCLUSIONS

1. Claude X. was of unsound mind at the time of the offences according to the criteria of Article 64 of the Criminal Code. He is mentally defective and his conduct is increasingly

marked by deterioration and seriously disturbed reactions to others, and he uses weapons irresponsibly.

2. This is therefore a case where mental disturbances may affect behaviour. He should be considered a danger to public order and to himself and confined.

AUTHOR'S NOTE

As the family environment is considered to be normal by the social enquiry and felt to be so by the boy, it is his lack of taste for school, lack of success there and his low IQ which here determine the diagnosis of mental deficiency. Nevertheless, as 'a defective of this level can normally live at home', the authorities fall back upon two other elements in order to justify their intervention: Claude 'spends his time amusing himself' and 'has the habit of vagrancy'. He must be made to re-adapt to discipline. How? He kills birds with a shotgun. He is 'a danger to public order and to himself': a formula taken from Article 64 of the Criminal Code and which requires official placement of the subject in a psychiatric hospital. This compulsory placement is supposed to bring Claude back to discipline and to 're-adaption to small tasks'. Later on, he will be able to go to an IMP with, suspended over his head to ensure his goodwill, the possibility of a return to hospital and, for good measure, financial supervision because he is mentally deranged.

PROBATION REPORT I

Subjects: Jean and René
born 21 July 19.. at Lille, and 30 November 19.. at Lille.
living with M. and Mme X. at Lille.

I have the honour of presenting the following report:

It was towards 11 o'clock when I arrived at the home of M. and Mme X., several children were playing in the room, Mme X. was busy preparing her meal. M. Z. was present.

M. Z. did not at first understand the purpose of my visit but nevertheless insisted emphatically 'that he is very pleased with his children at the moment'.

He assured me that he had not been drinking since leaving hospital, but I wasn't so sure of that judging by the smell of his breath.

The sister seemed to want to protect the children, she did not hesitate to take her father up on what he said and it was she who explained my presence to him.

According to his statements, Jean is working on a building site at the end of the street. René and Paul go to school; all is going well.

According to what the sister and father say it would seem that the children pose no problem.

In fact, despite the father's insistence that all is well, that Jean only goes to the cinema once a week and that he is as happy about him as about the others, we cannot be certain that the situation of the children is as desirable as it should be.

Incidentally, I learnt from Mme K., whose son is under a probation order and one of Jean's mates, that Jean very frequently went to seek refuge at her home, that most of the time he was untidy, and that nobody seemd to be bothering about him.

The father has been detoxicated. But when I arrived he was drinking beer, was dirty and unshaven, with untidy clothes. His speech was slow and he was finding it difficult to understand what was said to him.

I do not think he can be of much help in the upbringing of his children.

The sister seemed a good liar and is probably not as attentive as she wished to appear.

It seems to me that the best solution, if the family situation does not improve and if the boy is in agreement, would be to place Jean in a home for young workers in Lille to secure better material conditions of existence for him.

As to René and Paul, following the advice given by the vocational education consultation, it would be desirable for them to be able to benefit from a stay in a specialised establishment with the aim of obtaining for them a comprehensive, but closed, educational framework.

The probation officer for L.S.

PROBATION REPORT 2

Subjects: Paul born 20 March 19..

　　　　　René born 30 November 19..

I have the honour to present the following information concerning Paul and René, living with their sister Mme X. in Lille.

I have made many visits to the family since January; the welcome given to the officer is always very cool: it seems to be distrustful. The house is in poor repair and often in disorder (torn curtains, scattered heaps of linen).

M. Z. the father of the boy is always there, always sitting in the same place, unshaven. He wants to try to give a good impression. However, during my last visit, he drank three glasses of beer in less than a quarter of an hour, and he only responds to my questions by talking nonsense.

Mme X. replies to questions one puts to her but does not prolong the conversation. Nevertheless her replies are sensible. The number of people living at home seems beyond her control. And the living space is very cramped.

Paul and René go to school, Voltaire School. According to Mme X. they frequently play truant and she can't keep on their tail because of her housework and the other children. We have sought the opinion of the director of Voltaire School concerning these two children.

In June we were informed that Paul and René had little potential and that it would be necessary and in their interest to look towards a placement.

On 10 June we received a communication from the director of the establishment indicating that, following our letter, he immediately transmitted the information to the children's magistrate. He also enclosed copies of the school reports.

PAUL (C.E.2)

A very weak pupil, undisciplined, lazy, a thief, plays truant, unmoved by threats.
Average mark: 4.5 out of 10; twenty-fifth out of twenty-six pupils.

RENÉ (C.P.: REMEDIAL SECTION)

Work medium, undisciplined, a bad influence on the others, plays truant.
Average mark: 7.75; class position: first out of eight.

Mme X. hopes to be able to send her two young brothers to a holiday camp during the summer.

M. T., a student social worker with the children's court, had asked for advice on these children from Mlle N., the social worker in the outpatients' welfare department. Receiving no answer from her we repeated the request, whereupon she informed us on 26 May that Paul and René were not known to the department.

It seems in the present circumstances that, given the material situation of the family, the number of people living in the same house and the heavy responsibilities borne by Mme X., together with Paul and René's backwardness and their tendency to play truant, these boys could be made the object of a placement. For the elder, the Capreau Children's Home, for the younger, the COT Lambersart.

The probation officer for L.S.

IRREGULAR FAMILIES

The following report contains the essential details in the dossiers of two families taken into care by a children's court.

A. A SPECTACULAR CURE

19 December 1970. The preliminary police report:
'On 15 December 1970, at 12 o'clock, we heard it rumoured

that a child of the Leblanc family was taken to hospital on the evening of 12 December, after being found in a serious condition. Doctor P. confirmed that he had visited the young Raymond Leblanc.' (The police made enquiries at the chemist's to verify that the mother had indeed bought the prescribed medicines. She had done so, but in two batches, not having enough money to pay for them all at one time.) The Leblanc woman is unfavourably known to our services for her habitual frequenting of drinking establishments and her loose conduct. The day when the youngest Leblanc child was ill, Mme Leblanc was drunk. She habitually has extra-marital relationships.

Enquiry in various drink shops frequented by Mme Leblanc:
(1) Chez Mauricette: Mme Leblanc arrives every morning at 9.00 having taken the children to school. She consumes a half of draught beer and buys her packet of Gauloises cigarettes. In the afternoon or evening she will come back to drink three or four beers.
(2) Café la Jeunesse: two beers an evening, with her husband.
(3) Café la Scarpe: two beers a day. Here she often makes crude and vulgar remarks.[1]

Enquiry at the school: The headmistress: 'One of the Leblanc children has a weak constitution, often drowsing at her desk. Her breath smells of alcohol. When questioned the little girl has said that she drinks beer at the midday meal. The Leblanc children who are at nursery school frequently have to be sent home because they are dirty.'

Enquiry at the town hall: 'The bad reputation is confirmed. Nevertheless, M. Leblanc is a voluntary fireman and actively participates in social work. He is a CGT (Confédération Général du Travail: i.e. trades union delegate). The Mayor recommends that something should be done.'

Enquiry from the employer: 'A qualified, conscientious worker, but not very diligent'.

'Given the information collected above, we consider that we should proceed to obtain a social enquiry on this family.'
Composition of the family: father 33 years old, mechanic; mother 28 years old; six children aged between 9 and one.

Accommodation: 'The upkeep and cleanliness of the kitchen are more or less acceptable. In the bathroom, we noticed that the bathtub and washbasin were covered with grime. The lumber-room, where the dustbins are kept, is repulsively dirty. The parents' bedclothes are very dirty. The children's beds are equipped with decent sheets, very likely they had been changed the previous day. The garden is neglected. In front of the house the borders are well-tended.'

Financial resources: Father's salary between 800 and 1,000 francs per month.

Health: 'There is no family doctor, they call in any doctor, as the need arises. The cleanliness of the whole family is minimal. The maintenance of linen leaves much to be desired. At midday the meal consists of meat, vegetables and dessert. In the evening, only vegetables.'

Personality of parents: 'Leblanc Michel comes from a good background. Can read and write, no more. His conduct and morality attract no unfavourable comment. His intemperance is well-known. Although reliable, Leblanc is not diligent in the factory. He has no educative ability, not having much motivation. Leblanc Claudette bears out her reputation of drunkeness in her appearance. Her eyes are glassy. She looks at least 45. She can read and write. Her behaviour and morality are the subject of much gossip in Z., and the whole neighbourhood. She has no educative capacities.

2 January 1971.   Requests from the public prosecutor to the children's magistrate.

6 January 1971.   Provisional order of placement from the children's magistrate.

19 January 1971.   Letter from Mme Leblanc to the magistrate:

'I am venturing to write to you to tell you that my children were taken from me on 6 January on the grounds that supposedly I often leave my children alone in the house. But they were at school. The smallest is one year old. When I went to do the shopping, I had my neighbour close by, because the baby often sleeps. I don't understand, because my home is well kept and there is always suitable food. But I have another thing to say to you: there was a policeman who arrived at my home quite on his own to take photos of my rooms, and even look in my wardrobe. I believe that a policeman on his own cannot do this without warning us. Sir, I hope to expect a reply and to see my children again.'

25 January 1971. Letter from M. Leblanc's parents to the magistrate:

'I beg you to give back the children, because their parents have stopped eating. I pledge to you on our honour that the children will lack nothing. Have pity on two grandmothers and a grandfather who weep for their grandchildren, who need to give us happiness on Thursdays and Sundays.'

1 February 1971. The police, on the instructions of the children's magistrate, gave the grandparents to understand 'that having been given very bad information collected about the mother, there will be no question of returning the children.'

21 April 1971. Letter from Mme Leblanc to the judge:

'I would like you to send someone to my home to inspect the house, because all is in order to receive my children back home.'

23 April 1971. Order for a social enquiry:

2 June 1971. Letter from Mme Leblanc to the magistrate:

'I am venturing to write to you to ask you when my children will be returning.'

8 June 1971. Note from the social worker to the magistrate:

'Since the children were taken away the persons concerned have made a spectacular recovery: detoxication cure for the mother, fitting out and cleaning the house, and restoration of good relations between the spouses. In addition, the children have been regularly visited.'

Taking the children away seems to have created the necessary psychological shock to help them to get a grip on themselves and entirely reorganise their living conditions.

7 July 1971. Judgment:

'Considering that we learn from the social worker's report that the Leblanc couple have made a spectacular recovery: detoxication of the mother, fitting out and cleaning of the home and good relations between the couple ....'
Placement order lifted.

B. A DUBIOUS FAMILY

26 June 1971. Police report and preliminary enquiry:

Following many interventions made by our services at the house of the Delatre couple, a social enquiry on the family and its environment was decided upon: five children, all minors aged between 8 years and eighteen months: Gonzague, Georgette, Gérard, Xavier, Georges.

Environment: In an old converted farmhouse. The general aspect of the house is not spotless.

Resources: Salary of Delatre, driver, 2,000 francs per month plus 630 francs family allowance.

According to Mme Delatre's statement, her husband only gives the household 800 francs per month for reasons which we have not established.

Nevertheless, Delatre, having been sentenced to pay 2,324.26 francs in fines, repays the sum of 500 francs monthly.

No debts contracted, but the shopkeepers of the *quartier* distrust this family.

Personality: father is never present in the house through his duties as lorry driver. The mother is without taste, lacking direction. Father of doubtful morality. Appears to have contracted a slight venereal disease a year ago. Has been the object of legal proceedings:

–in 1968 for abduction of minors without deception or violence;
–in 1968: failure to register lodgers;
–in 1968: social enquiry;
–in 1968: traffic accident;
–in 1968: invalid driving licence;
–in 1969: issuing unsupported cheques;

–in 1969: involuntary wounding and evading arrest.

Mother of doubtful morality, likes to receive young people in her home. According to the husband, disappeared from home for several days at the end of the past year. Father well thought of by his employers.

Leisure: No television, no means of distraction existed in this home. However, we have, on a number of visits, noticed Mme Delatre and two of her sisters dancing with young people in the courtyard of the residence, to the sound of a transistor.

Children: the children are untidy in their clothing. We note, however, that they must be decently fed because none of them is thin. No school absenteeism.

The family has not a very good reputation among the local food retailers. Furthermore, this family has the reputation of harbouring shifty young people who it sometimes knows to be sought by the police services. Frequent visits by certain young girls and youths who come to seek refuge have been noted. Yet the place has nothing to encourage sensible young people to come to reside in the house.

Conclusion: a measure of particularly strict supervision with regard to the Delatre wife. Guardianship of family allowances.

Finally, it appears opportune to intervene firmly in this environment which is disturbed by the bad behaviour of the mother who, quite shamelessly, allows idle young couples to gather in her home to hold 'parties' there and act in an immoral fashion.

Up till now, the advice which has been dispensed to the Delatre wife, notably by ourselves, has changed nothing in the attitude of this person who does not understand that the health, both physical and moral, of her children, is in particular danger.

9 August 1971. The procurator requests an intervention by the children's magistrate.

16 August 1971. AEMO order for three months.

12 September 1971. Report of the police enquiry indicating that the Delatre couple have been advised of the proceedings opened against them.

19 May 1972. Social enquiry.

Father's salary: 1,600 francs (*not* 2,000 francs), plus 650 francs family allowance.

The father, although working regularly enough as a lorry driver (it is his only source of income, but with different employers), is considered as a person of little standing, though from a respectable family; he has been well brought up, but by his marriage to Paule C. has contracted a sort of misalliance which perhaps explains in part the failure of his home life. Appears intelligent enough, but unstable. He presents himself sufficiently well to deceive the people around him.

He gives himself up to loose living, and although he is not a true alcoholic, to drink. He admits to having had mistresses, and to having one still. His excuse is his dislike of his home resulting from his wife's misconduct and uncleanliness. The excuses can in fact, to a certain extent, be taken into consideration, but nevertheless they do not explain the number of proceedings against M. Delatre – for morals, for unpaid bills and for driving offences.

For these reasons Gonzague Delatre is a man known to the police. But, impenitent recidivist that he is, he opposes any improvement by simple inertia or else, under the cloak of his fairly amiable appearance, seeks to pose as a victim of bad luck, of fate, of marital problems, etc.

As for the mother she is an entirely different type, considerably inferior. Coming from a mediocre working-class family (careless in conduct and morals, a habitual tendency towards excessive drinking, brings the children up badly), she seems to have nothing in common with her husband: the sort of loose character which makes her consider her own faults as excusable (or even non-existent). So here we are running up against stubborn and unreasonable incomprehension. Paule Delatre's only reaction is to complain bitterly about her husband's behaviour, especially towards herself. In the course of our visits, we have often heard her complaining in tears about her husband's infidelity, refusing to see that, if he were received into a neater house, he might perhaps be more faithful.

Disorder and dirt in the home, and poor care of the children, are without importance in the eyes of this young woman, given that the children are in good health. The truth is that Mme Delatre is lazy and dirty. Her intelligence is minimal and she seems incapable of sound judgement. She amuses herself at home in the company of youths and young girls. Everyone drinks, sings, dances to the music of records, and meanwhile, of course, the children are extremely neglected.

The family gathers most of the time in a dark kitchen, where dilapidated and dirty ceiling and walls combine to give a grim appearance. Disorder and uncleanliness everywhere. Dirty crockery, piles of dirty clothes on the chairs and on the floor.

M. Delatre works regularly, but always gives very little money because of his court orders and also because of thoughtless expenses such as a recently acquired, superb television set, which occupies a place of honour in the middle of the slum.

In consequence of all the above, we ask for the AEMO measure to be renewed for two years, together with a serious reprimand for the Delatre couple.

We suggest guardianship over social benefits.

16 June 1972. Judgment (The Delatre parents do not appear.)

AEMO order for three years.

The preliminary police enquiry is accompanied by providing the magistrate with a sheaf of photographs taken on the spot.

7

THE PRODUCTION OF
DESTRUCTION

The delicacy and minuteness of analysis are themselves an effect of nostalgia.   (Jean Baudrillard, *Cublier Foucault*, Galilée, 1977)

Each wave which you produce reduces the variety of forms which a human being can assume.
     (John Brunner, *Sur l'onde de choc*, Robert Laffont, 1977)

The progressive destruction of society by the State, the organisation of towns as spaces in which to conform, the predation upon and ordering of communal space by the public authorities, the imposition of a way of life based on supply and demand, the classification of the masses into standardised families, the systematic hounding of those who are irregular, handicapped, incapable or rebellious have ended up by producing within the social fabric the model of the family as we know it today.

Why should this model be the final one, why should it and indeed how can it be the supreme achievement, the ultimate stage in the dislocation of society by the State?

From the time of La Reynie to our own day, the public space has not ceased to expand and the structures that mediate between the State and individuals meanwhile have become increasingly scarce. Hardly had the Haussmann operation reached the peak of its achievement than it began to appear old-fashioned: once Paris – and, following its example, many other towns too – had been entirely emptied not only of its *plebs* but also of its proletariat, society lost not just its streets but its towns as well, for these have, in their turn, now become no more than places for traffic to pass through.

Haussmann's successor, nowadays prefect of both the Ile de France and Paris, gave some indication of what the urban scene of the future will be when he proposed 'abandoning the term "towns" which implies walls and limits, in favour of the term "agglomeration", linked by fast connecting motorways'.[1]

Crossed by the two urban motorways and two railways, north–south and east–west, by-passable thanks to a circular route, itself flanked by a ring road 64 kilometres long connected in its turn by exit routes to a secondary road 94 kilometres long, the Paris of the last quarter of a century has become insignificant, in the middle of a network of tight chainmail made up of fast highways running between the various poles of employment on the one hand and housing on the other. Paris will become, in fact, no more than an agglomeration, a concentration of narrowly defined functions and, when that happens other places will follow suit.

Everywhere streets give way to 'highways', to specialised traffic, to homogenous circuits, without it being possible for this change to occur without affecting the whole environment. There are urban motorways, riverbank roads, radials, link roads, cycleways, pedestrian streets, shopping centres, each with its own rhythm, its own destination, its own relationship with the environment.

The indefinable spaces are all disappearing, giving way to ones with definitive functions. Spaces for work, for sleeping, for leisure, for walking, for social or commercial exchange, for traffic, for pausing, for a returning to nature or for absorbing culture, all provided with their own forces of animation and control: military bandsmen, and policemen in the metro, pedestrian streets and state security agents in the Latin Quarter, promoters of free expression and security agents in the Pompidou Centre, conservation and rules and regulations in nature reserves.

Beggars, musicians, singers, photographers and bill-stickers are absolutely forbidden along these paths. It is forbidden to form any group or assembly of a type which might obstruct passers-by, to walk or sit on the lawns, to play an instrument, to repair or clean cars, to beat carpets or cushions, to damage or strip trees, to pick flowers, to climb trees, to walk along the edges or banks of the lakes, to set up any equipment against the trees to bathe in the lakes and rivers; likewise to place any boat or engine thereon, including models supplied with internal combustion engines, without permisson, to scare the water birds, to perform any action which might in any way disturb other people's peaceful enjoyment of the park, to offer free services to the public.[2]

When towns have been gutted in order to facilitate the movement of traffic, their centres, from then on uninhabitable, are occupied only by an elite of authorities who exaggerate and commercialise all the outward signs of byegone urban life, and of the old town relationships. But above all, these centres are occupied by administrative and economic headquarters, by vast leisure complexes, by huge administrative edifices with different social functions, by all the symbolic iconography of the State. The remainder of the town is scattered on a periphery, the limits of which roll back unceasingly, dispersed or regrouped in 'New Towns'. Almost every part of the entire space is increasingly directly prescribed with a special function.

On top of the rules and constraints of the urban continuum there are those of the buildings in which people live. 'Plans for communal buildings will be formulated with the idea of avoiding any occasion for encounter between tenants, the open landings and stairways will be considered to be extensions of the public highway. Corridors and passageways must rigorously be pronounced out of bounds whatever the cost.'[3] The rule of separation between families remains the absolute prerequisite of all policies for workers' housing. 'When Monsieur Claudius-Petit asked the bosses who were building the housing why, instead of providing a place for a washing machine in each apartment, they did not contemplate creating one wash-house, laundry and drying-room per building, they told him that it was not prudent to bring different households together with the risk of spreading political propaganda and increasing trades union membership.'[4]

As well as this policy of discouraging too much communal space, there are the multiple effects of a policy of industrialisation, and thus for the standardisation of housing, which makes it impossible to escape the same intractable concrete walls and the same plaster-block dividing ones, incapable of taking the weight of a nail. The framework of life is dictated once-and-for-all, and in the most minute detail: the entry points of water, gas, electricity, telephone or joint television aerials, connected with networks encased in the walls, pre-condition the allocation of the different rooms, their use and even their furnishing. No divergence of function can be made in any of these except by violence, deceit or fraud, and any such deviation would constitute at the very least a sign of non-integration, vulgarity and strangeness.[5] It would inevitably run foul of the controlling authorities and caretakers who are charged with imposing a respect for the programmed utilisation of space and the, frequently minute, rules of cohabitation, covering the rhythm of life, noise, hours and modes of using shared places; and there are decrees which regulate the drying of linen, the walking of dogs, the repair of cars and the play of children. Misuse of the habitat, which is to say misunderstanding or transgressing these multiple rules, necessarily attracts the attention and provokes the intervention of those managers of 'deculturalisation', the social workers.

The car parks and cellars may become places where groups of young people gather; the stairways, lifts and corridors may be used as something other than simple 'extensions of the public highway', lawns may become playing fields and housing estates mission fields. And if they can they all do, given that the restricted possibilities offered by the public space and the structured framework can only produce the most minimal kind of sociability, a non-habitat, in which the resident has no active relationship with, or right of intervention in the environment, only basic users' rights, the forms of which are prescribed and abundantly codified in the multiple regulations.

This impoverishment of the relationship to the environment accompanies a similar impoverishment in people's relationships to work and to their needs. The concentration of production in a few large complexes and the limitation of distribution to a few large networks, the rise in the level of capital necessary for either kind of enterprise and the degree of centralised management which they require, leave room only for rationalised and artificial kinds of know-how and lifestyles and for a synthetic culture.

After a certain point, Taylorism and the distribution of tasks are necessary elements in processes of production and above all in their control since, the higher the worker's qualifications, the more he constitutes an obstacle, a possible source of contradiction to the central rationale. Work is limited to the repetition of finely divided tasks, the purposes and ends of which remain mysterious to the performers. The worker is an atomised producer, as are the managers of public enterprises and public services, employees and civil servants.

The indispensable imposition of products prepared at the cost of considerable investment entails the increasingly refined development of a technology of people's needs, making it possible to control an ever-expanding commercial space and turning every vital activity into a possible or probable merchandise. The satisfaction of needs becomes as artificial and dispersed an activity as that of production. The consumer, downgraded into a 'target', is constituted by a sample, taken *in vitro*, of the lowest common denominators in certain categories selected from the social fabric, on the basis of the particular characteristics that they display, and then arbitrarily given identities. Age, status, income, sex are thus each considered in isolation and arbitrarily assigned distinctive needs. Economic engineering selects its own field in which to operate and defines categories of people with a purely imaginary existence. The regrouping of these dissociated categories into a super category, constituted by the family, provides a framework for the technology of needs, by appearing to substitute a social unity in place of the atom necessary to mass consumption. But it is also because this technology of needs crosses, carves up and divides the family on many occasions and in many ways, that the latter breaks up, losing the instrumental functions assigned to it by the nineteenth-century organisation of society.

It has long been the exception for families to practise a

common trade, and this absence of the productive role of the family unit goes along with the disappearance of any economic function. Patrimonies have been undermined by the speed of inflation. Anonymously managed by specialised establishments, they are transformed at best into simple liquid assets and can no longer play their former role of offering some kind of refuge – a possibility of mutual aid in the face of disaster. The insurance programmes and institutions of social security now monopolise the exercise of solidarity.

Family self-sufficiency is everywhere a thing of the past. The disappearance of the garden means the family cannot produce its own food; home-made clothes have been replaced by less expensive factory-made items, which are more varied and made popular through advertisements; all kinds of domestic services and self-help have been rendered useless through the mass-production of objects designed to be replaced rather than repaired when damaged. In a context in which 'no one produces what he consumes or consumes what he produces'[6] the family does not possess any economic viability on its own.

The centralisation of distribution and the introduction of technical and mechanical expertise in the sphere of household activities entails their complete dependency.

In 1977 the proportion of purchases made in France by 'major' or 'centralised' commerce rose to one-third of all retail purchases. Although previously confined to indispensable products, today this new means of distribution extends to almost the entire range of goods offered on the market and has now massively infiltrated the service sector. Automatic management of its stocks and orders is facilitated by the fastest possible circulation of a small number of products. It becomes possible to standardise consumer needs through the elimination of any goods designated as marginal. This favours mass production by a small number of producers, who concentrate their financial resources upon advertising, and offering credit, and advantageous terms of supply etc.

The consumption of mass-produced goods in a mass production framework gets the better of the family's role as the satisfier of needs and disqualifies it as a potentially original unit in the elaboration of a way of life. When tins and convenience foods replace fresh products, when packaged goods take the place of culinary skill, the table which was not so long ago a holy focus for families of all classes, is replaced by the refrigerator: each individual family atom turns to that for his or her ration, for whatever he wants whenever he wants it.

Dispersed in a habitat that has lost all vestiges of its territorial character, all ties dissolved, relieved of any economic function, with all sense of belonging rooted out, what basis can families find upon which to preserve order or to enhance their own autonomous ways of life? What practices, what particular ways of living, what habits can they transmit? What activities can they pursue outside perimeters marked out by the official places of knowledge, of consumption, of production, of health, of culture, of play?

The organisation of all social and economic exchanges and, likewise, the ordering of urban space are leading to the total impoverishment of sociability. The resulting paradox is surely that the family, which was until recently a satellite of the State, designed and used by it, is now becoming an obstacle to the State's total invasion of civil society? The family, the residue of a communal life as exhausted as soil can become, is a unit where State apparatuses have cleaned away and continue to clean away the smallest signs of profusion, exuberance and even neighbourliness. Is it not the case that now in its turn, this very unit has come to represent a form of sociability which is still too dense not to form an obstacle to the institutionalisation of all forms of life?

The steadily increasing strength of professional experts on how life should be lived and the corresponding widening of the field of their activities[7] are certainly, in many cases, still related to the family-oriented social work we have described above and much of the behaviour of these colonialisers of society still reflects what they have learnt from the conquerors who prepared the way for them. But if one examines tendencies already at work and the latest innovative trends in social work, does it not appear to be engaged in establishing itself not around apparatuses of support for family life but around institutions designed for the direct management of the social mass as a whole on the one hand, and of individuals taken in isolation on the other?

The trend for the ultimate function of families, that of raising children, to be taken over by these institutions is already well-advanced. Only one 3 year old child in two is still raised entirely by its family. One-fifth of the rest are raised directly by the State in placements for misfits of all kinds, about one-third spend the day within an 'educational framework' (crèche, nursery school etc.) and one-half is looked after by child-minders, official or 'unofficial'. But whatever the mode of education, the recommended official and scientific pedagogical methods affect not simply those children growing up in institutions but many others too.

In families on housing estates and in large complexes, this pedagogy is instilled by the social services at family allowance offices. Theoretical knowledge about childhood reaches the child-minders – now known as nursery school assistants – by way of policies of professionalisation much acclaimed by our modern versions of Jules Simon and accompanied by the inevitable distribution of diplomas. In short, the official line on the state of childhood, how it should be developed and its different stages and dysfunctions is purveyed to everyone through the press, specialist journals, radios, their advice programmes and 'phone-in' broadcasts and television.

When families in housing estates and large complexes ask the family allowance office for help which the break up of their environment has prevented them finding in neighbourhood solidarity, it is granted to them on the terms of leonine contracts to which I have already referred: the concession of a financial allocation – called exceptional (for the sick, the infirm, the apprentice, for prize-winning mothers, for a lay-ette,[8]) despite the fact that it may, like a housing allocation, concern one French family in six or, like 'holiday payments', concern 1,200,000 children – in return for the social services' right to intervene in any families requesting such grants. Neither these services, nor those of the departmental management of health or social work require any warrant or legal authorisation to intervene in these families. For the assumption by which they are affected is no longer that of irregularity or excess, but of incompetence and deprivation. In order to remedy this incompetence, the social workers organise instruction on how to live. Thus, in the last six months of 1976 the family allowance office of the Paris region organised a many faceted programme, which started by focusing on the raising of children: 'the management of the child's room, toys, the child's snacks, drinks, the minding of children, a six-week session of baby-sitter education in collaboration with the *maisons des jeunes*, allowing interested young people to be initiated into the fundamental ideas of infant welfare and psychology.[9]

The same programme also provided for mothers to learn how to make curtains and bedspreads; the arrangement of the appartment, the choice of household appliances, a simple and rapid method of filing forms for family allowances, social security, taxes etc., the purchase, choice and upkeep of linen; quick cookery; balanced diet; removing stains from linen; cooking up left-overs; ... the problems of drugs, the problems of the adolescent.[10]

What social work does not win from the families through the blackmail of financial aid, it acquires by emphasising its capacities and monopoly in the matter of health. The obligation to declare a pregnancy to the Mothers and Children Protection Services (PMI),[11] makes it possible to set up a system of testimonials that can be exploited by an information system. This exploitation leads to the constitution of a population of children who are 'at risk' or considered 'supervision priorities'. The following are some of the social criteria that allow the information programmes to trigger off intervention in the family by a social service:

the profession of the recipient or of the mother (if he or she is): an agricultural wage-earner, a minor, an apprentice, a manual worker, a charwoman, a student or school pupil, a conscript, a former agricultural worker, or a person without a trade;

the foreign nationality of the mother, where the trade is one of those mentioned above;

an age under 18 or over 40;

the number of pregnancies in excess of:

2 if the mother is less than 21
3 if the mother is less than 23
4 if the mother is less than 26
5 if the mother is less than 28
6 whatever the mother's age.[12]

For the poorest families, the criteria are lower based and the service on offer is 'a housing allocation [which] is only one part of a whole in which instruction, professional training, instruction in housekeeping, hygiene, child welfare and intellectual influence play equally important roles.[13] This policy of overall aid provides for encouraging families to sign 'contracts of occupation' which stipulate that the leaseholder undertakes 'not to occupy his housing except with members of his family and any possible children yet to be born ... to allow the sanitary authorities, the health service workers or any accredited person to visit his housing at any time ..., not to make any alterations to the state of the place ..., to air it appropriately to avoid condensation ..., to avoid anything which might be prejudicial to the wellbeing and reputation of the place ...[14] etc.

Child-minders or nursery assistants, about 500,000 in number, of whom only 200,000 are known to and accredited by the child social welfare services, have a professional standing which is still not fully organised. The programme for their training is therefore still at an elementary stage as is shown by the brochure published by the Ministry of Health entitled 'L'Enfant et sa famille d'accueil' ('The child and its foster family'), in which child-minders are informed of the most frequently manifested symptoms of a child's adaptive difficulties: lying, stealing, running away, bed-wetting, sexual problems, educational failure' and are counselled to respond with 'discretion, to avoid dramatisation, and to talk it over with a social worker'.

The obsession with the family, characteristic of the old tradition of social work, becomes not only archaic but also contradictory to this direct management of the child's upbringing, in which all private activity is referred to public economy and an ideal of behaviour. To be sure, the family subsists, at least formally, as long as the union of a man and a woman is necessary for the conception of a child. But this generative function seems to be the last one left to it in the State's programme for the direct manipulation of individuals. And even that function is subject to reservations: the conception and expectation of a child are a subject for official pedagogy and theoretical knowledge. The inclusion of sexual education into the school curriculum is accompanied by the creation of groups for pregnant women who are taught, by the family allowance office and social services, how to live with their condition, while it is further hoped in future to organise groups for their partners, where the latter will learn the correct scientific way to treat pregnant women.

Things which not long ago were subject to harassment or penalisation – divorce, abortion, contraception, individualism, change or mobility – are today considered unimportant, or as no more than the province of particular institutions. In so far as it is the State which produces and manages cultures and ways of life, individuals disappear behind the delegated functions which they exercise, but which someone else could equally well exercise in their place. Prohibitions and taboos are reduced in number and intensity, in exact proportion to the extent to which their transgression can be administered by public powers. Abortion is permitted, not as an act freely decided upon by a woman, but as an action the motivations for which must fall into a statistical category defined by the law and recognised to be in conformity with the canon of the only kind of health which remains, namely public health.

In monopolising the organisation of communal life in order to establish officially what is good for society, the State is involved in a constant work of pauperising sociability – of exterminating society. The elements that provisionally led to

the constitution of the family, have now been superseded by
the atomisation of that unit, at once so weak and yet still too
impenetrable. Thus any attempts to produce a communal life
outside the field of the institutions, any attempt to regain
initiative, any dissidence against the universe of protection,
every effort to enable society to reclaim the role of actor and do
its own gardening, constitute so many manifestations of resistance to the possible destruction of society by the State, so
many instances of opposition in face of this outrageous possibility becoming an inevitable doom.

NOTES

I. FAMILY REGULATIONS

1 Philippe Ariès, *Centuries of childhood* (Harmondsworth, 1973).
2 Ibid.
3 René Descartes, *Philosophical writings: a selection* (Nelsons University, 1971).
4 Translator's note: there used to be a 'Court of Miracles' in every large town: in the seventeenth century there were about a dozen in Paris. The best-known description is that given by Victor Hugo in *Notre-Dame de Paris*. These areas were places which the officers of the watch would enter at their own discretion voluntarily. Relatively silent by day, by night they became noisy and unruly. They offered asylum to those who wished to evade the law, and had their own rules and hierarchies. The one described by Victor Hugo was cleaned out in 1656, and the inhabitants sent to hospitals or prisons. The town reconstructions of the nineteenth century destroyed their last vestiges.
5 On φιλειν 'to love' and αδελφρς 'brother', Restif de la Bretonne, *Les Nuits de Paris* (1788).
6 M. Guillante, Officer of the Ile de France mounted police. Report submitted to the King 1749, entitled *Mémoire sur la réformation de la police en France*.
7 Jeremy Bentham, *The Panopticon* (Belfond, 1977).
8 Ariès, *Centuries of childhood*.
9 Translator's note: Pierre Antoine Berryer (1790–1868). Advocate and parliamentarian known for his openness to modern ideas, despite his avowed royalism.
Antoine de Sartine, Comte d'Alby (1729–1801). Lieutenant General of the Paris Police 1759–79. Responsible for cleaning and lighting the streets of Paris.
Jean Charles Pierre Lenoir (1732–1807). Unpopular and severe Prefect of Police and magistrate.
Georges Eugene Haussmann, Baron (1809–91). Prefect of the Seine 1853–70. His name is connected with the transformation of Paris. Under his grandiose planning the city took on its present

123

form. He was concerned with public order and cleanliness, removed former working-class and revolutionary areas and slums and built the present straight boulevards.

Louis Lépine (1846–1933). Administrator and Prefect of Police in various departments, concerned particularly with traffic planning.

Jean Chiappe (1879–1940). Prefect of Police 1927–34. Right-wing administrator and Vichy Government supporter. Town councillor of Paris 1935, and Deputy for the Seine 1936.

10 Cross-section of a four-storey house made by Karl Giradet December 1847. In *Le Parisien chez lui au XIXième siècle* (Archives Nationales, 1976).

11 'Behold in the same room, a father working, a mother occupied with household details and children who, depending on their age, either play or are beginning to help those who brought them into the world.' L-G. Montigny, *Le Provincial à Paris* (1825).

12 Albéric Second, in *L'Univers illustré*, 13 (12 July 1860).

13 Account of the tenants of the building situated at 23, Rue Blondel; in Giradet *Le Parisien chez lui*.

14 Martin Naduad, *Mémoires de Léonard, ancien garçon maçon* (Hachette, 2nd edition, 1976).

15 Translator's note: Ange Guépin (1805–74). Doctor and left-wing politician. Author of *Traité d'économie Sociale* (1835).

Jean Paul Alban Villeneuve-Bargemont, Vicomte de (1784–1850). Administrator and economist. Prefect in various departments. Author of *Economie politique chrétienne ou Recherches sur les causes de paupérisme* (3 vols., 1834).

Louis René Villerme (1782–1863). Doctor and sociologist. In 1837, he was charged by the Académie des sciences morales et politiques with the task of studying the French poor. Author of *Tableau de l'état physique et moral des ouvriers dans les fabriques de coton, de laine et de scie* (2 vols., 1840), which was influential in the formation of nineteenth-century social welfare law, particularly the 1841 law on working children.

16 Roger Caillois, extract from his 'Prèface à l'exposition Paris et les Parisiens au 19eme siècle'.

17 The present 'grands boulevards'.

18 In addition to these four Free Towns, the villages of La Chapelle, La Villette, Belleville, part of Saint-Mandé, Bercy, part of Ivry, part of Gentilly, part of Montrouge, Vaugir and Grenelle, Auteuil, Passy and Les Ternes were annexed. The area of Paris was increased from 3,370 to 7,802 hectares, and its population from 1,174,346 in 1856 to 1,696,141 in 1861. See *Histoire de Paris et*

des Parisiens (Collected essays) (Éditions de Pont-Royal, Paris 1958).

19 Joseph Lefort, *Étude sur l'amélioration et le bien-être des classes ouvrières* (1875).

20 Joseph Lefort, *Du repos hebdomadaire* (1877) (footnoted 'the secret of working-class morality lies in a Sunday day of rest'). Prize essay for the Académie des sciences morales et politiques. (See *Statistiques de l'industrie de Paris*, first part, p. 71.)

21 Henri Baudrillart, *Rapport àl'Académie des sciences morales et polituques*, reprinted in the preface of Lefort, *Du repos hebdomadaire*.

22 On these points, particularly the pursuit of the unmarried and the authorities' obsession with stability, see Lion Murard and Patrick Zylberman, 'Le petit travailleur infatigable ou le prolétaire regénéré', *Recherches*, 25 (November 1976).

23 *L'Ouvrier de huit ans* (Librairie Internationale, Paris, 1867).

24 See Pierre Jakez Hélias, *Le Cheval d'orgueil* (Plon, 1975); also the increasingly numerous autobiographical publications which, it should be stressed, refer to culture in terms which would have been laughed at no more than fifteen years ago.

25 Ariès, *Centuries of childhood*.

26 Albert Dussenty, 'Le vagabondage des mineurs' (thesis in law, Toulouse, 1938).

27 Armand Mosse, *De l'application des lois relatives à la préservation et à la protection des enfants en danger d'abandon moral*; report to the Committee for the Defence of Children Brought before the Law in Paris (Melun, Official Publication, 1937).

28 Félix Morin, 'Des comités de défense des enfants traduits en justice' (thesis in law, Toulouse, 1879).

2. THE REALM OF OFFICIAL RECOGNITION

1 Édouard Ducpétiaux, *De la condition physique et morale des jeunes ouvriers, et des moyens de l'améliorer* (Brussels, Meline, Lang et Cie, 1843).

2 *Cf.* Christian Paultre, 'De la répression du vagabondage et de la mendicité sous l'Ancien Régime' (thesis in the faculty of law, Paris, 1906).

3 Translator's note: all the citizens of the empire must follow the customs of the city.

4 Ducpétiaux, *La condition physique*.

5 Morin, *Des comités de défense des enfants*.

6 Joseph Rozès, 'Les Enfants vagabonds; des remèdes préventifs et répressifs à apporter au vagabondage des mineurs de seize ans' (thesis, Toulouse, 1900).

7 *Revue de l'Éducation surveillée*, 4 (1946).
8 *Rééducation*, First Quarter, 117–18 (1960).
9 *Ibid.*

3. THE STATE: HOME OF THE FAMILY

1 Decree of 20 April 1684. There was no limitation on the age for the imprisonment of girls.
2 Laws of 25 September 1792 and February 1793.
3 It rose from 215 to 1,044.
4 Report to His Majesty the Emperor by His Excellency the Minister of the Interior; 1852, Paris, printed by P. Dupont, 1854.
5 *Ibid.*
6 Renouard (essayist, member of l'Institut de France).
7 Jules Simon, *L'Ouvrière* (Paris, Hachette, 1861).
8 Jules Simon, *De l'initiative privée et de l'État en matière de réformes sociales.* (Lecture delivered at Bordeaux, 1892.)
9 Lefort, *Du repos hebdomadaire.*
10 Michel Foucault, *Discipline and Punishment* (Allen Lane, 1979).
11 Simon, *De l'initiative privée.*
12 Lefort, *Du repos hebdomadaire.*
13 Translator's note: Dr Jean Marc Gaspard Itard (1775–1838), Physician of the Institute of Deaf Mutes.
14 Meeting of the General Society for Prisons on 15 February 1899.
15 *Ibid.*
16 Mosse, *De l'application des lois relatives.*
17 *Ibid.*
18 *Cf.* Jean Animard, *Étude sur l'oeuvre de l'union française pour le sauvetage de l'enfance;* (thesis, Montpellier; printed in Marseilles, 1929).
19 Paul Virilio, *L'Insécurité du territoire* (Stock, 1976).
20 George Orwell, *Nineteen eighty-four* (Harmondsworth, 1966).

4. IRREGULAR CHILDREN AND THE POLICING OF FAMILIES

1 Translator's note: Joseph-Marie Dégerando, Baron (1772–1842). Philosopher, politician and writer on the education of deaf mutes. An administrator who had a successful career under the Empire.
2 Hélène Campinchi, in *Rééducation*, 1 (March–April 1946).
3 *Ibid.*
4 *Ibid.*
5 *Ibid.*
6 J.L. Costa, the first Director of Supervised Education, in *Rééducation*, 5 (September–October 1946).
7 In 1970, the hourly minimum wage was 3.27 francs, which for a week's work of forty-two hours would correspond to a monthly wage of 600 francs.

8 This was a family of eleven children, living in five rooms. The father was a total invalid and the family received 1,960 francs a month from invalidity pension and social security.

9 Translator's note: the doctors Diafoirus (father and son) were characters in Molière's play *La Malade imaginaire*. They were opposed to new-fangled ideas like Harvey's discovery of the circulation of the blood. All the doctors in this play show a superstitious reverence for the dogma and rituals of their profession, rather than an ability to deal with present circumstances.

10 Except in cases where the infraction committed is a crime against persons (nil in Lille in 1973) or against property (ten out of 1,570) and for cases where an infraction incurring a major penalty has been committed. In these two cases recourse to an examining magistrate is compulsory.

11 By this procedure, the department for public prosecutions gains direct control of the legal sentence without going through the intermediary of examination. The procedure for cases of *in flagrante delicto* is similar.

12 *Cf.* Methodological note made by the direction of Éducation Surveillée, March 1974.

13 *Cf.* p[97].

14 For practical reasons (the lack of such reports in the court statistics) and for reasons of time, it has not been possible to study the proportion of minors cautioned and subsequently sentenced before they reached the age of majority.

15 *Cf.* p.100: a report by a probationary officer.

16 R. Jamin, 1903. 'Du droit de correction patternelle' (thesis in the faculty of law, Paris, 1903).

17 See Pierre Leulliette, 'Un assassinat exemplaire', *Esprit*, 3 (1977).

5. INDIVIDUAL CASES UNDER SCRUTINY

1 An organisation run by ex-alcoholics.

7. THE PRODUCTION OF DESTRUCTION

1 Press conference of the prefect of the Ile de France, Prefect of Paris on 13 May 1977, in *Bulletin d'information sur Paris et la région parisienne*. No. 12, Association Region Paris Presse.

2 Paris Prefecture Decree of 25 February 1977 concerning the general regulation of the streets of the town of Paris, including the Bois de Boulogne and Vincennes; in *Bulletin d'information de l'ARPP*, No. 8.

3 Motion adopted at the International Congress on Cheap Housing. Paris, 25–28 June 1889.

4 *Combat.* 12 January 1952, cited by Louis Houdeville, *Pour une civilisation de l'habitat* (Editions ouvrieres, Paris, 1969).
5 *Cf.* the current 'rumour' which has it that Algerians use their bathrooms for rearing goats and sheep.
6 Michel Bosquet *Écologie et Liberté.* (Éditions Galilée, Paris, 1977).
7 *Cf.* 'Pourquoi le travail sociale', *Esprit*, 4–5 (1972). (Reprinted in 1975.)
8 In 1973 social benefits (all payments taken together) represented 20% of the gross revenue of households.
9 Family Allowance Office, Paris Region, report concerning the activities of family economy and mutual aid. (Private collection, 1977).
10 *Ibid.*
11 Law of the 15 July 1970.
12 *Cf.* CFDT (Trades Union). *Informatisation du secteur sanitaire et sociale.* Brochure published by the Paris Regional Union of CFDT. April 1976.
13 Ministry of Works Circular, nos. 66–15, 13 May 1966, on the clearing of shanty towns.
14 Ministry of Works *Pour une politique concertée du relogement et d'action socio-éducative appliquée à la résorption des bidonvilles*, May 1967. (The complete text of the agreement runs to seven pages of single-spaced typing.)